# PERSONNEL PLANNING GUIDE

*Second Edition, Revised and Expanded*

A handbook to help you and your small business with
**personnel management.**

**Upstart Publishing Company, Inc.**
The Small-Business Publishing Company
12 Portland Street
Dover, NH 03820
Telephone: 603-749-5071
Outside of NH: 800-235-8866

Publishers of:
*Business Planning Guide*
*Personnel Planning Guide*
*Market Planning Guide*
*Cash Flow Control Guide*
*Common Sense Management Techniques*
and other publications for small-business owners

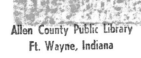
# About the Author

David H. Bangs, Jr. is President of Upstart Publishing Company, Inc., which he founded in 1977. As developer of the company's product lines, he authored the *Business Planning Guide* (which has sold over 100,000 copies), the *Personnel Planning Guide*, the *Cash Flow Control Guide*, the *Market Planning Guide* and over 30 *Common Sense Management Techniques* topics.

Prior to founding Upstart, Mr. Bangs honed his business-management and communication skills. He was coordinator of the Business Information Center in Exeter, New Hampshire, a pilot project for a Federal Reserve Bank of Boston regional economic development plan. For several years, Mr. Bangs was a commercial loan officer at Bank of America in Los Angeles, where he worked with small high-tech businesses. At the University of New Hampshire, Mr. Bangs taught courses on logic and the philosophy of science.

Mr. Bangs lives in Portsmouth, New Hampshire with his wife, Lacey, and two of their five children.

Published 1986. Second edition 1987.

Library of Congress Catalog Number 86-050982

Published by:    Upstart Publishing Company, Inc.
                 Portsmouth, New Hampshire  03801

ISBN 0-936894-00-8

# Table of Contents

# To the Reader

The examples used throughout the *Personnel Planning Guide* are based on my experience as a banker, consultant, and most importantly, as a small business owner for 10 years. Some are drawn from Upstart, some from conversations with my friend and partner Steve White, and some from our network of small business experts (writers, bankers, Small Business Development Centers, and others). Special thanks go to Bill Scott, Professor at the University of New Hampshire's Thompson School of Applied Science. I've drawn heavily on work he has done for Upstart, and especially on his GRAPE theory (see Chapter Eight for details).

My aim is to provide you with a set of tools and instructions on how to use those tools. The forms and checklists are there for your use—feel free to copy them. Alter them to fit your needs—they are tools, not commandments chiseled in rock. And as with any set of tools, the more you use them the more proficient you become.

They are simple, basic tools—hammers and chisels and screwdrivers—that work. For fancier tools (tablesaws, routers, and so on), check the Bibliography in the Appendix. There are many good texts which expand on the techniques offered here.

Each chapter is divided into three parts: the major concerns; ways of dealing with them; and forms and examples based on real businesses. If you need help with a specific problem, such as how to fire someone, turn to the appropriate chapter. You may find that dealing with some problems takes a lot of preparation—and paperwork. There are compelling legal reasons for this: Check with your lawyer. Fill out the forms, follow the steps, and use your judgment. We know that these forms and processes work. They'll work for you, too.

If you find that you need additional assistance, ask for it. There are many sources of information and assistance ranging from the SCORE program of the Small Business Administration, to Small Business Development Centers (SBDCs) at various state universities, to local business assistance programs. Check them out.

The best way to use this book is to read through it, use whatever personnel tools and techniques are most immediately applicable, and then set down a personnel management plan that addresses the needs of your business for the future. Managing a business is hard enough without running headlong into avoidable problems.

Plan ahead. Plan what's going to happen.

Then make the plan happen.

David H. Bangs, Jr.
Portsmouth, NH
June 1986

# Foreword

*I decided to reprint the following letter as testimony to the many ways the* Personnel Planning Guide *can help you manage your most valuable resource.*

*—Editor*

 CORNERSTONES-WRIGHT,INC.

10 Danforth Street, Portland, Maine 04101                    (207) 772-3900
Mailing Address: P.O. Box 4904 DTS, Portland, Maine 04112

March 31, 1987

The Editor of Upstart Publishing Company
Upstart Publishing Company, Inc.
50 Mill Street
Dover, NH   03820

RE:   Personnel Planning Guide

      Congratulations!

      I have been using a copy of your Personnel Planning Guide
for the past six months and have found it to be so useful that I
decided to write and tell you about it.

      I am President of a specialty engineering software house,
which is built on the team of people that we have put together.
The company was recently reorganized by merging with its parent
company and moved to a new location with new management.
Recently, we addressed all of the classic start-up problems as
well as the organizational changes associated with a move, new
president, etc.  Since Cornerstones-Wright's success is
dependent on our people, (2/3 of our expenses are personnel), it
was critical that the transition be smooth.

      Our first focus was in getting the new company legally
established.  Your listings of legal responsibilities and checklists were indispensable in that process.  Maine has its own
forms, declarations, licenses, and registrations as well as all
the Federal requirements.

After being established as a legal business, it was time to address the organizational structure and individual responsibilities. Cornerstones-Wright fortunately maintained time records which made job analysis and writing job descriptions straight forward in conjunction with your outline. We were able to reallocate some of our people's effort and improve our productivity without adding any new people.

With job descriptions in hand, we established goals for each individual in the company and used them to review their past year's performance. Using the present to review the past is not fair but better than fuzzy qualitative measures. Once again, your outline, forms, and procedures worked exceptionally well. We kept all of our employees except for one who we had to release. Because the separation was for cause, we followed your documentation approach and the process went smoothly, without any repercussions.

This must sound like a parrot speaking. Everything that the Personnel Planning Guide said to do, we did. The payoff will not come for five years when our sales are $10,000,000. The PPG has helped our company establish a firm foundation in managing our people. Speaking personally and for my business, your Personnel Planning Guide is well worth the $16.75 I paid for it. I have never seen anything equivalent in my 25 years of experience or six years of college at both the undergraduate and MBA business levels.

I would recommend the Personnel Planning Guide to any and all business owners or managers who need to understand the fundamentals of good personnel management. Having used your Business Planning Guide for years in my previous consulting business, I expect to do the same with the PPG.

Keep up the good work and let me know when you decide to develop any other guides - I want to buy them.

Sincerely,

G. William Eldridge
President
Cornerstones-Wright, Inc.

# Introduction

Why is personnel planning so important to your business?

Let's say you have five employees and one of them is a dud.

That's 20% of your work force.

That dud interferes with everyone else—griping and slouching around upsets other workers and makes them uneasy. Say their productivity is reduced by 25%—a conservative estimate when you have a troublemaker on staff. A 25% reduction in productivity per person, times four people, equals another person.

That makes 40% of your work force unproductive. In a company with 500 employees, that would mean 200 non-performers, a condition that wouldn't be tolerated for a minute. Yet that state of affairs is by no means unusual in small businesses.

Why?

Probably because small business owners tend to race around putting out fires, doing work that their employees should have done, solving problems that could have been avoided.

Managing people—beginning with selecting new employees—is difficult. Personnel management in large companies is a skilled specialty, but in your small business you have to be the skilled specialist—usually without much, if any, training. Most personnel manuals and textbooks are geared to the needs of companies with hundreds of employees.

So were do you start? Just reading this handbook sets you apart from your competitors. Apply the practices and procedures outlined in the following chapters, fill in the blank worksheets provided in Appendix One—and don't hesitate to call for help if you need some.

Employees are the most important asset of your business. They are also the most expensive. You can't depreciate employees—in fact, they want more pay every year. If they are unhappy, they quit—at the least convenient time. You then have to replace them, train and orient their replacements, pick up the slack during the training period, provide benefits, and even (in many cases) continue to pay the employee who left. Work flow is disrupted, making the remaining employees less productive until new routines are established. You have to spend added time with the new employee. The costs are high.

Payroll costs are the highest fixed cost in almost every small business. According to representative trade ratios published by Dun & Bradstreet, Robert Morris Associates, and other financial reporters:

## Payroll Averages

| Type of Business | Percentage of Gross Sales |
|---|---|
| Retail | 6.2% |
| Wholesale/distribution | 3.0% |
| Manufacturing | 8.0% |
| Services | 11.1% |
| Communications | 15.7% |

In contrast, rent averages less than 2% of gross sales across the board. And note that these are averages—for many businesses, the payroll cost is much higher. These averages do not include benefits, which average 30% of payroll.

Personnel problems come in a number of disguises. The more common ones are:

- ☐ High turnover
- ☐ Absenteeism (especially on Monday or Friday)
- ☐ Tardiness
- ☐ Goldbricking
- ☐ Low productivity
- ☐ Increased accident rates
- ☐ Excessive waste
- ☐ Poor quality control
- ☐ High customer complaint and/or reject rates
- ☐ Machine problems
- ☐ Downtime
- ☐ Poor morale

Can you do something about these kinds of problems?

Sure. Make sure you have the right employees, properly trained and equipped, in the right positions.

That's what this handbook is all about. If you are willing to allocate the time needed to prevent and cure personnel problems, your business will be more fun to run and profits will increase. No magic. No secrets.

Just carefully apply your efforts. Personnel management is more than a clerical task. It's the essence of management—and requires close attention to details and implementation of the well-tried processes in this book.

The example used in this book is based on our own experiences at Upstart Publishing over the past 10 years. We asked several companies to be our example and they declined—on legal advice—which in itself illustrates the growing difficulties of personnel management.

Hire properly, and you'll avoid most personnel problems. The most common cause of personnel problems in small business is overly hasty hiring—followed by choosing employees from too small a pool of qualified applicants.

You can successfully compete for and retain good employees. A small business has many advantages, starting with close working relationships and communication with your employees. Larger companies have to carefully plan ways to approximate some of the benefits small business owners take for granted (or don't notice at all). Among these are:
- Growth opportunities (for individuals);
- Recognition of successes;
- Achievement, in the company and in the community;
- Participation in management and other work-related decisions; and
- Efforts by management (you) to clearly and consistently communicate company goals and challenges.

Put these to work for your business. Use the forms and checklists, and use the Upstart examples as guides to creating your own personnel policies and practices—and you will minimize your personnel problems.

# Chapter One:
# What Are My Legal Obligations
# As an Employer?

Your legal obligations as an employer are in flux. The "employment at will" doctrine is being rapidly eroded by both state and federal courts. Equal Opportunity laws have an effect on how you recruit, hire, promote and dismiss employees.

State laws concerning employment practices vary—but as a rough rule of thumb, you are obligated to treat all job applicants fairly and equitably regardless of their race, color, religion, sex, or national origin.

Some people are panicked by this and long for a mythical time when employers could hire whomever they wished, fire them whenever they felt like it, and in between these times, treat employees whimsically.

More rational employers simply want to proceed with business, comply with the laws, and be legally protected. Lawsuits, no matter how groundless, are increasingly popular—perhaps because there are too many lawyers, perhaps because there is a lot of confusion about what constitutes an employee's or an applicant's rights.

What can you do to protect yourself? For a start:

☐ Be familiar with the basic legal obligations you bear as an employer. Some of them are listed in Figure 1.1 on the next page.

☐ Whenever there is any doubt—as in terminating or suspending an employee—do not hesitate to call your lawyer.

☐ Take advantage of the information available to you from the US Department of Labor, the Wage and Hour Division of the US Department of Labor, the National Labor Relations Board, the EEOC (Equal Employment Opportunity Commission), State Labor Departments and Human Rights Commissions, and the IRS. They have a wealth of information and advice for you, and will show you how to comply with the regulations. For free.

☐ Don't try to sail too close to the laws. Many employers get into legal problems by being too smart: not withholding Social Security and income tax payments, ignoring minimum wage or overtime laws, exercising personal prejudices.

☐ Keep accurate, dated, written records: for hiring and recruiting, for promotions and evaluations, for disciplining and terminating, and for otherwise dealing with problem employees. The burden of proof against charges of discrimination will be on you—and few defenses are stronger than well-documented evidence that you have made, and continue to make, a good faith effort to comply with the law.

**Keep accurate, dated, written records: for hiring and recruiting, for promotions and evaluations, for disciplining and terminating, and for otherwise dealing with problem employees.**

1

Figure 1.1

# Employer Obligations

| Obligation: | Basic Requirements: |
| --- | --- |
| **Federal Income Taxes** | ☐ Get IRS Form SS-4 for employer's identification number.<br>☐ Give new employees or employees changing the number of exemptions a W-4 (Employee's Withholding Exemption Certificate).<br>☐ Deposit withheld taxes according to IRS schedule on IRS Form 501.<br>☐ File Federal Payroll Tax Returns, Form 941, each quarter.<br>☐ Give employees completed W-2 forms at end of the calendar year. |
| **Social Security Taxes (FICA)** | ☐ Obtain employee's Social Security number and withhold required percentage of wages from paycheck; contribute equal amount; deposit and report on IRS Form 501 (see above). |
| **Federal Unemployment Tax (FUTA)** | ☐ Contribute and deposit percentage of employee's wages as required.<br>☐ File IRS Form 940, Employer's Annual Federal Unemployment Tax Return, on or before January 31. |
| **State Unemployment Tax** | ☐ Check with state authorities; ask your accountant. Varies from state to state, and from industry to industry. |
| **State Unemployment Insurance** | ☐ Check with state authorities; ask your accountant. |
| **Workers Compensation** | ☐ Check with your insurance agent. You must provide your employees with insurance coverage for job-related injury or accidents. Coverage may be obtained from the state or from private plans approved by the state. Varies state-to-state and for workers in different occupational classes. |
| **Employee Benefits** | ☐ See Chapter 11; check with your accountant to make sure your pension plan complies with ERISA and subsequent legislation. |
| **Federal Wage and Hours** | ☐ Pay minimum wage; time-and-a-half for more than 40 hours a week; comply with child labor regulations. Retain basic payroll records and documentation of time worked. |
| **State Wage and Hours** | ☐ Check with your state's agency (Labor, Industrial Relations)—their regulations may differ from federal regulations. |
| **EEOC (Title VII)** | ☐ If you have 15 or more employees: "Treat applicants and employees fairly and equally regardless of race, color, religion, sex (including pregnancy), or national origin in all employment practices including hiring, firing, promotion, compensation, and other terms, privileges and conditions of employment." |

| | |
|---|---|
| **Equal Pay Act of 1963** | ☐ Equal pay for equal work for both men and women. |
| **Age Discrimination** | ☐ If you have 20 or more employees, treat applicants and employees equally regardless of age. The law specifies the 40 to 70 age group. |
| **Employer with Federal Contracts or Subcontracts** | ☐ Prohibits discrimination in employment on the basis of race, color, religion, sex, or national origin. Covered employees must take affirmative action to hire and promote protected groups, qualified handicapped people, Vietnam-era Veterans, and disabled veterans of all wars. |
| **OSHA: Occupational Safety & Health Act** | ☐ Provide safe work place; comply with OSHA occupational health and safety standards. |
| **Local Fire Department** | ☐ Ask your local fire department for a compliance check on exits, stairs, location of fire extinguishing equipment, and so on. |
| **Employment Eligibility** | ☐ Verify employment eligibility on Form I-9 as required by Immigration and Naturalization Service. |
| **Posting Requirements** | Somewhere in your work place, you may have to post: |

☐ Fair Labor Standards Act
☐ Title VII of the Civil Rights Act
☐ OSHA bulletins
☐ Office of Federal Contract Compliance equal opportunity regulations
☐ Payday schedule
☐ Safety and health regulations
☐ Worker's Compensation carrier notice
☐ Unemployment and disability carrier notice
☐ Holiday schedules

---

As a summary, you have a duty to your employee to:

☐ Pay for work performed;
☐ Refrain from discriminating in pay, promotions, benefits, and working conditions because of the employee's race or sex, color, religion, or national origin, union activity or membership.
☐ Provide a safe working place free from recognizable hazards to the emloyee's safety or health.
☐ Make required contributions, on schedule, for Worker's Compensation, Unemployment Insurance, and Social Security.
☐ Make required deductions and deposits from employee's pay for income tax and Social Security payments.
☐ Comply with federal, state and local laws covering other aspects of employment.
☐ Comply with the terms of any employment contract with the employee or with a union representing the employee.

For an excellent short book covering the rights and obligations of employers and employees, we recommend *The Law of the Workplace* by James W. Hunt, available from the Bureau of National Affairs, Inc., Washington, DC, © 1984. ISBN: 0-87179-446-2.

Some businesses are exempt from some of the requirements sketched in Figure 1.1—but don't assume that yours is one of them. Check it out with your lawyer. Family businesses and businesses employing fewer than ten people are exempt from some federal requirements, but may be subject to state requirements covering the same areas. Check first, and check periodically. Laws change. So does their interpretation.

The best defense is to comply with the laws and treat all employees fairly, equitably, and consistently. Try the Golden Rule as a guideline: Treat others as you would have others treat you. While it can't guarantee you against an oddball lawsuit (nothing can), it will go a long way towards showing good faith in your dealings with employees.

Throughout this book reference is made to a principle of fairness. This principle asks that you treat all applicants and employees evenhandedly, play no favorites, establish clear and consistent policies and communicate them to your employees. Fairness does not demand that you hire anyone who applies—you can and should be discriminating in your choice of employees, and choose those persons you think are best matched to the requirements of the job.

Fairness cuts two ways. As an employer, you are entitled to fairness, too. The personnel practices suggested in this book will help you get the right worker for the job, allow the workers to produce for you, and even help you discipline or fire unwilling employees. The law does not require you to be a social agency, a charity, or a philanthropy.

It does demand that you be fair. That really is no hardship. Treat your employees fairly, and they'll treat you fairly. Assume that they want to work and do a good job; provide the environment, tools and training, and they will. Most of the time. There will be the occasional employee who tries to take advantage of you—but even there, you can treat the person fairly. You may have to fire him or her, which can be done cleanly, fairly, and legally if you follow some straightforward procedures.

Figure 1.2

# Record Retention Checklist

**Two Years**
- ☐ All general business correspondence.

**Three Years**
- ☐ Bank statements and deposit slips;
- ☐ Payroll time sheets;
- ☐ Purchase orders;
- ☐ Sales records.

**Four Years**
- ☐ Expired insurance policies.

**Five Years**
- ☐ IRS Form 8300: Report on cash transactions over $10,000 received in a trade or business.

**Six Years**
- ☐ Personnel records;
- ☐ Income tax returns;
- ☐ Dividend checks;
- ☐ Expense reports;
- ☐ Accident and fire insurance reports;
- ☐ Subsidiary ledgers;
- ☐ Monthly trial balances;
- ☐ Correspondence regarding licenses, purchases, shipping, and receiving.

**Eight Years**
- ☐ Payroll checks;
- ☐ Earnings records;
- ☐ Canceled checks;
- ☐ Production correspondence;
- ☐ Group disability insurance reports;
- ☐ Insurance safety reports;
- ☐ Expired mortgages, notes, and leases.

**Ten Years**
- ☐ Settled insurance claims.

**Permanently**
- ☐ Audit reports;
- ☐ General ledgers and journals;
- ☐ Permanent corporate records: charters, bylaws, corporate minutes books, stock and bond records;
- ☐ Cash books;
- ☐ Copyrights and patents;
- ☐ Contracts;
- ☐ Deeds;
- ☐ Proxies;
- ☐ Retirement and pension records;
- ☐ Working papers;
- ☐ Canceled checks for taxes, property purchase, and contracts.

As a rule of thumb: Keep records as long as this chart indicates—or longer. You may have to document a claim or substantiate a tax deduction, and need these records.

# Chapter Two:
# Do I Need Another Employee?

Adding an employee is a major undertaking.

Sometimes the need is obvious: A key employee quits or retires, leaving a void. A sales increase is coming. Maybe you have a good employee who wants to do something else—still in your business—but that leaves a gap. Or you find that quality is sliding because you don't have the right workers available at the right times, so every job becomes a rush job.

Your employees are your business' most important asset—and their payroll is the largest single fixed expense. Compared to the cost of even one employee, equipment tends to look cheap.

What costs are involved? Salary, FICA (Social Security), various unemployment and worker's compensation insurance. Additional fringe benefits. Training and orientation. Disruption of current work flow until the employee is fully productive. The total is alarming.

For example, compare the costs of buying a $25,000 machine and hiring a full-time employee for $15,000 a year.

|  | **Machine** | **Employee** |  |
|---|---|---|---|
| Downpayment (30%): | $7,500 |  |  |
| Annual Cost: | 6,975 * | Salary: | $15,000 |
| Upkeep: | 2,500 | FICA etc.: | 1,500 |
| Insurance: | 500 | Insurance: | 1,200 |
| Total: | $17,475 | Total: | $17,700 |

*Based on a three-year amortization, 12% interest.

That's just the first year, with no "downpayment" (training and opportunity costs) and no benefits allocated to the new employee. In the second year, the picture is even more striking:

|  | **Machine** | **Employee** |  |
|---|---|---|---|
| Annual Cost: | $6,975 | Salary: | $15,000 |
| Upkeep: | 2,500 | FICA etc: | 1,500 |
| Insurance: | 500 | Insurance: | 1,200 |
| Total: | $9,975 | Total: | $17,700 |

Please note that you didn't give the employee a raise. Now think of the last employee you hired, and the last major equipment purchase you made. How much time did you take with each decision?

**Never hire anyone without a good business reason.**

## Pre-Planning: Personnel Plans and Business Plans

The most basic rule for any personnel policy is: Never hire anyone without a good business reason. To do this, tie your personnel plan to your business plan, that is, to the overall goals which you set for your business.

Why write up a personnel plan?

- ☐ To prepare for change;
- ☐ To be ready to replace retiring employees;
- ☐ To prepare for other departing employees;
- ☐ To compete for—and retain—good employees;
- ☐ To avoid last-minute hires for critical jobs;
- ☐ To protect your cash flow; and
- ☐ To minimize fixed expenses.

---

Figure 2.1

**Personnel Pre-Planning Questions**

- ☐ What personnel do you have now?
- ☐ What are they doing? Have the tasks been timed?
- ☐ Can their jobs be restructured to accommodate projected growth?
- ☐ Do you maintain a skills bank (a listing of the skills and training of your employees)?
- ☐ Can overtime be used to avoid a new hire?
- ☐ If no overtime is currently being paid: Why not?
- ☐ According to your business plan, what will your personnel needs be in six months? One year? Five years?
- ☐ What replacements do you foresee?
- ☐ What critical jobs might have to be filled?
- ☐ What is the replacement time—recruiting, orienting, training—for these jobs?

---

Unexpected departures do happen. What would happen if your best salesperson quit in a huff and went to work for your biggest competitor? Or your best tool and die man decided to move across the country?

Your business plan is concerned with what-if questions of this kind. You want to avoid surprises as much as you can. Replacing key people can be easily overlooked as a potential problem.

At least once a year, write down your answers to these questions for each critical position (including your own):
- ☐ What has to be done to replace _____?
- ☐ What lead times are needed?
- ☐ What training time is involved?
- ☐ Where would I find a replacement for _____?

Try to list at least five sources—perhaps your files, employment agencies, vocational schools, referrals from current employees.

Then form a backup plan. The ideal replacement is hard to find, and the longer you plan ahead the better.

If you raise questions here that you can't answer, don't worry. That's the point of this exercise. Look for options now, when you aren't under the gun. Compare alternatives, ask for advice from your banker, accountant, other business owners, friends.

## Pre-Planning: Listing Tasks

What tasks have to be done in your business? A rough list helps you identify the ongoing tasks—open the door, turn on lights, check the shelves for stocking before customers come in...turn out lights, close and lock door... You want to list these carefully so you can allocate them to your employees.

Most tasks fall into one of four categories:
1. Daily
2. Weekly
3. Monthly
4. Occasionally

Use Figure 2.2 and jot down the tasks as they occur to you under the appropriate heading. It takes time to do this thoroughly—some of the tasks will be overlooked the first few times through.

Some of the tasks will involve more than one person. Sometimes this is necessary. One person can't handle the job alone, some cooperation and socializing on the job is an important element of employee morale, or the timetable demands cooperation. Sometimes many hands do not necessarily mean light work, and the disruption of other tasks adds to the time wasted.

Your aim in Figure 2.3 is to get a handle on those tasks that take more than one person. It isn't to squeeze 2,400 minutes of productive time out of each employee each week. A secondary aim is to help you establish norms for tasks and projects that get repeated periodically. You need norms—time records of how long a task should take—to improve productivity, prevent too much employee slack time, and run your company profitably.

You need norms—time records of how long a task should take—to improve productivity, prevent too much employee slack time, and run your company profitably.

9

Figure 2.2
# Task Listing

| | Frequency: | | | |
|---|---|---|---|---|
| Task: | Daily | Weekly | Monthly | Other (specify) |
| 1. Open doors | ✓ | | | |
| 2. Sort/distribute mail | ✓ | | | |
| 3. Do daily bookkeeping | ✓ | | | |
| 4. Take care of telephone sales | ✓ | | | |
| 5. Counsel employees | | | | as needed |
| 6. Make coffee | ✓ | | | |
| 7. Visit customers | | | | at least quarterly |
| 8. Talk with clients | | ✓ | ✓ | |
| 9. Talk with prospects | | ✓ | | |
| 10. Prepare monthly statements | | | ✓ | |
| 11. Review sales figures | | ✓ | ✓ | |
| 12. Check inventory | | | ✓ | |
| 13. Set type; prepare C:Ms | ✓ | | | |
| 14. Service machinery | | | ✓ | and as needed |
| 15. Meet w/ all employees | | ✓ | | or biweekly |
| 16. Set and review marketing plan | | | ✓ | and quarterly |
| 17. Make telephone sales | ✓ | | | |
| 18. Write articles | | | ✓ | and as needed |
| 19. Prepare re:Posts C:Ms | | ✓ | | |
| 20. Write copy fr re:Posts | | ✓ | | |

Figure 2.3
**Large Tasks**

Name of Task: _prepare Re: Posts_

People Needed: _JEK, AK, LB, BH, JMK, SR, interns_

What They Do: _Set and proof type, prepare C; Ms for Wednesday evening delivery to printer, edit copy, layout ads, etc._

When They Do It:   ☐ Daily   ☑ Weekly   ☐ Monthly

   ☐ Other (Specify) _____

How Many Hours
Does It Take:   _Average to date: 45 ± /week_
   _Aim for 35/week_

Total Time (by Individual
or by Task):

|   |   |   |
|---|---|---|
| ① Typesetting | 20.0 |
| ② Paste up, layout | 20.0 |
| ③ Proof | 2.0 |
| ④ Edit | 6.0 |
| ⑤ Bookkeeping | 2.5 |
| ⑥ Delivery ; miscellaneous | 2.5 |

_53 hours total (last week)_

Comments:

_Need to speed up ① and ② ; suggest salespersons get ads in sooner; prepare standard format; check with publishers of other periodicals for bright ideas._

11

**You have to make sure that your employees spend their time (your money) productively.**

Do these for all the tasks or projects that take more than one person's time. You may want to set an arbitrary limit, say any task taking more than six hours or occurring more than once a month, to limit the paperwork at first. Once you establish norms, and improve performance, this management tool will become indispensable.

Now collate the times (roughly) by week, by employee. Parkinson's Law that "Work expands to fill the time allotted" is especially hard on small businesses. You have to make sure that your employees spend their time (your money) productively. You cannot do that without knowing in detail how they now pass their working hours—and how they should be passing them. You need facts, times, and more facts.

Use the information gained in Figures 2.2 and 2.3 to fill in Figure 2.4.

When you go over these sheets, keep asking yourself:
- ☐ Who should do this job/task?
- ☐ Do they have enough time? Too much time?
- ☐ Could it be better scheduled?
- ☐ Does it have to be done at all?

You may find that another employee isn't needed, that you can reschedule and coordinate your current employees' efforts more productively.

You may find that you do need to add another person—and now you have a well-defined set of tasks for that person to perform. Keep these lists of tasks—you will need them for Chapter Four: Job Descriptions. And make sure you hire:
- ☐ Only for a clear need;
- ☐ To increase profits;
- ☐ For justified replacement; or
- ☐ For planned growth.

If you have any doubts, don't hire. Postpone the decision. Consider the alternatives:

- ☐ Part-time help (including apprentices or interns);
- ☐ Contract the work out;
- ☐ Using a temporary agency;
- ☐ Using a consultant.

Figure 2.4

## Employee Time Use Form

Name of employee: ___BH___

| | Mon | Tues | Wed | Thurs | Fri | Sat/Sun |
|---|---|---|---|---|---|---|
| 8:00 | Open up → | | | | → | |
| 8:30 | set up typesetter → | | | | → | |
| 9:00 | check chemistry | | Proof re: Posts | Training and | Typeset projects | |
| 9:30 | meeting | paste-up | | practice Mac | | |
| 10:00 | Typeset | | | | | |
| 10:30 | | | | Paste-up | | |
| 11:00 | | | | | | |
| 11:30 | ↓ | ↓ | ↓ | ↓ | ↓ | |
| 12:00 | Lunch → | | | | | |
| 12:30 | | | | | | |
| 1:00 | Typeset | Typeset C5 | Typeset C5 | Bulk mail | Postage run | |
| 1:30 | | | | | ↓ | |
| 2:00 | | | | | Change | |
| 2:30 | | | | | Chemistry | |
| 3:00 | | | | | | |
| 3:30 | ↓ | ↓ | ↓ | ↓ | ↓ | |
| 4:00 | Shut down Typesetter → | | | | | |
| 4:30 | | | | | | |
| 5:00 | | | | | | |
| 5:30 | | | | | | |

Fill out this form (and have your employees fill them out) for several weeks. A word or two should be enough to describe how the time is being used—or a task number, if you numbered the tasks in Figure 2.2.

13

# Chapter Three:
# How Is Time Really Spent?

Your quickest personnel management payoff comes when you budget time for management functions.

A large business has specialists for each management function. In your business, you have to fill the role of several specialists. Maybe all of them.

Use Figures 3.1 and 3.3 to make sure that each area is covered. A profitable business is one where all of these functions are covered—not brilliantly perhaps, but adequately.

Make sure that each area is assigned to an individual. That person—you or a colleague—should then examine how the time is actually being used. Keep a time diary (such as Figure 2.4), noting how you actually spend your time. Otherwise, you can only become more efficient by chance.

**Keep a time diary. . .noting how you actually spend your time. Otherwise, you can only become more efficient by chance.**

Figure 3.1
**Managerial Worksheet**

| | Person Responsible | Hours/Week Actual Proposed | | Hours/Month Actual Proposed |
|---|---|---|---|---|
| Planning: | AB | 2-3 | | 10 |
| | JW | 2-3 | | 10 |
| Organizing: | AB | 2-3 | | 10 |
| Staffing: | JEK | 2 | | 10 |
| Supervising: | JEK | 5 | | 25 |
| Directing: | JEK | 10 | | 40 |
| | SW | 5 | | 25 |
| Controlling: | SHW | 10 | | 45 |
| Coordinating: | (? PROBLEM AREA!) | | | |
| Innovating: | AB | 8 | | 40 |

Combine the results of Figure 3.1 with a look at how your business is organized. If you don't have an organization chart, make one.

A simple organization chart (Figure 3.2) for a small company might include the following positions:

---

Figure 3.2
**Standard Organization Chart**

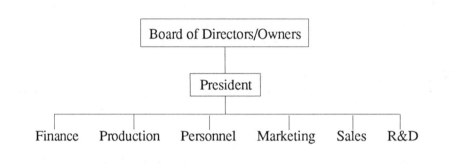

---

Other areas—Distribution, Purchasing, Administration are examples—may be important in your business. The important thing is to make sure that no major position is left uncovered. A single person—you—may be filling all of these positions, or you may be sharing or delegating duties.

But an individual, whether you or a trusted employee, has to be responsible for these duties. A job assigned to everybody (or assigned by default) is a job assigned to nobody—and is a job that won't get done. That kind of omission murders small businesses.

Top management—you—has duties above and beyond those shown in Figures 3.1 and 3.2. New business development, public relations and advertising, succession planning, and setting long-term goals are duties that don't fit into most charts.

Figure 3.3

# The Managerial Functions

1. **Planning:** Set objectives, allocate resources, establish strategies to attain objectives. Set benchmarks to measure progress, and set tactics (action plans) to make the strategies effective. Determine resources needed: capital, equipment, plant, personnel. Special plans needed include financial, marketing, and personnel plans.

Some basic questions to raise include: Where is the business going in the next three years? What challenges and opportunities do we face? What resources do we have—and what do we lack? What markets do we want to enter, abandon, dominate?

2. **Organizing:** Work backwards from the objectives and forward from the present to determine what tasks have to be done, when, by whom, and with what resources to attain the objectives.

3. **Staffing:** Assign the right person to the right job. Make sure that someone is available for each necessary task. In small business, staffing is often done ad hoc: "This has to be done! Quick, get someone here to do it or I'll do it myself..."

4. **Supervising:** Observe your employees and check that duties are being performed effectively. Train to make sure skills are up to the tasks. Upgrade the work whenever possible to retain good employees. Supervision takes a lot of time, and while your employees are adults who need little supervision, they need some guidance and coordinating. Otherwise productivity will slip and performance evaluations become impossible.

5. **Directing:** If routines are impaired or disrupted, decisions about what to do have to be made. Ideally, this is rare—but it's very gratifying to put out fires, so many owner/managers spend far more time directing than makes good business sense. Let your employees direct their own work as much as possible; it helps them grow, gives you a better work force, and lets you spend your time more profitably.

6. **Controlling:** The basic control systems—Operations, Financial, Accounting and Bookkeeping, Personnel Management—call for timely, factual information routinely gathered and analyzed for deviations from the norms set in your planning and managing efforts.

**Companies having difficulties *always* lack at least one major control system.**

7. **Coordinating:** Making all the parts and people in a business work in concert towards common goals is a task worthy of a maestro. Marketing and finance have to harmonize; distribution and sales need to keep the same time. Think of the maestro conducting the orchestra: coordinating, timing, scheduling, prompting, and keeping all performers focused on the same score.

8. **Innovating:** Allocate time to pay attention to the future of your business. If you leave the future to chance, your competition will clobber you. What new products, new technologies, new ideas will affect your business in the next several years? People who look for opportunities find opportunities. It's a management responsibility.

Figure 3.4
**Daily Management Tasks**

A small business owner wrote us: "As a business owner, I have five things to do every day. To make sure I do them, I use the following form. It helps the rest of my business even if I only think about these things."

| Day/ Time | Seek Opportunities | Plan | Organize | Measure | Improve |
|---|---|---|---|---|---|
| Mon. | | | | | |
| Tues. | | | | | |
| Wed. | | | | | |
| Thurs. | | | | | |
| Fri. | | | | | |
| Sat. & Sun. | | | | | |

**Time and Task Analysis**

What tasks are being performed now, by whom, and when?

Return to the listings of Chapter 2, Figures 2.2, 2.3, and 2.4. Reexamine them, observe your employees' actual performance, and get actual times.

This is not a judgmental step. Don't look to improve any particular task at this stage. Some can be improved, some will not be worth doing, others will be done about as well as possible. Solicit your employees' advice. Most employees want to do their jobs well, but if the jobs have been poorly planned or coordinated (your fault, not theirs), all the zeal in the world can't help.

What you want here is a listing:

"First, I set up the lathe. That takes half an hour. Then I get the turnings from the bin over there in the corner. Ten, fifteen minutes. The production run takes two and a half hours. Coffee break in there somewhere—fifteen minutes. Lunch. One hour. Set up for the next run and check the lathe, blades and so on. Half hour. Production run, three hours. Coffee break, fifteen minutes. Shut down and clean the machinery, return stock to the bin or put it on the dolly. Twenty minutes or so." You could get more details if you want, but this would be enough to start with.

Your employees are full of ideas and information about their jobs—how to improve them, change them, speed them up. Think of jobs you've had in the past—if you had one where the boss wanted your input, it was a good job, while if the boss dictated what you could do when, it was a lousy job.

You can help your employees with Figure 3.5: Task Analysis by gently directing them: "When you get here, what do you do first? Then what?...I see. Then?..." and so on. If there are more than 10 tasks, use another sheet. At this stage you should begin to examine each job for improvements or changes. A good rule of thumb is: If a practice has remained unchanged for a year, it's out of date and needs to be reexamined.

Figure 3.5
**Task Analysis**

Position: Office Manager     Date: 6/18/86

| Task | Time Spent Now | Suggested Revisions | Estimated Revised Time |
|------|----------------|---------------------|------------------------|
| 1. Mail | ½ hr. | Open once a day; have intern help sort, open, stamp | 15 min. |
| 2. Fill Orders | 1½ hr. | Have intern help so OM can have more time on computer | ½ hr. |
| 3. Daily Bookkeeping | 4 hr. | By using the computer, time will decrease | 3 hr. |
| 4. Answer Phone | 1 hr. | Get someone else to do this when OM is using computer | ½ hr. |
| 5. Learn New Computer Programs | 2½ hr. | Need more time! | 3½ hr. |
| 6. Help with Bulk Mail | ½ hr. | Can be a problem some times | 0 |
| 7. Errands: Coffee, Postage machine, etc. | ½ hr. | Has to be done | ½ hr. |
| 8. Making Telephone Sales Calls | 1 hr. | OM would like to do more! | 2 hr. |
| 9. Type letters | ½ hr. | Computerize letters to reduce time | 0 |
| 10. Order supplies; work w/ Vendors | ½ hr. | Order monthly, not weekly | 1 hr./mo. |

19

## Improving Time Use

You need a calendar (large, with lots of room to write on), a supply of Weekly Time Planning Schedules (Figure 3.6) , and a daily things-to-do list. Most time management systems are extrapolations on these simple tools.

The idea is to concentrate on the most important—not necessarily the most pressing—tasks. What do you want to accomplish in the next quarter or six months? That's where the calendar helps. Set down your goals, then work backwards to identify those tasks you have to perform to get to those goals.

Now break the tasks down into the Weekly Time Planning format. List the problems/objectives for each week. Keep the list short—10 problems or objectives a week is enough for anyone. This helps establish priorities; the undone list at the end of the week tends to get attention.

A daily things-to-do list breaks the larger jobs into manageable bits, ensures that appointments are kept, and provides a helpful record of what you did (and when) for IRS and other purposes. The daily entries should be related to the problems and objectives for the week—a handy check on what you do first.

Your input makes these forms valuable. They can give you a lot of information, especially in retrospect when you see what tasks you postponed or let slide. They help you spend your time more profitably—if you use them.

Figure 3.6
**Time Planning Schedule**

| Name _____ Week Ending _____ | |
|---|---|
| Problems/Objectives | Schedule |
| | Monday _____ |
| | _____ |
| | Tuesday _____ |
| | _____ |
| | Wednesday _____ |
| | _____ |
| | Thursday _____ |
| | _____ |
| | Friday _____ |
| | _____ |
| | Saturday _____ |
| | _____ |

What should be done—and by whom?

The time management puzzle is almost solved—and with it, a definitive answer to "Do you need another employee?" is closer.

After listing and timing all the major jobs in your company, ask of each one:

*Why do this particular task at all?*

If there's a good reason—and normally there will be—look for ways to improve the work flow.

Some questions to ask:

- ☐ Who is doing this?
- ☐ When? Where? How?
- ☐ Could someone else do it better?
- ☐ How can it be done better? (Organizing, coordinating, staffing? New equipment? Training? Farm it out?...)
- ☐ How do other companies handle this job? (You can always learn from your competitors.)

Look for big improvements first. Delete a task, combine it with another job, reorganize, reschedule, or simplify it to gain a big improvement.

The same goes for your own time use. Small business owners open the mail, balance the checkbook, run errands to "spare the secretary"—and ignore management tasks. Ask yourself the tough questions: Who should be doing this—me or someone else? When? Why do it at all?

## Create Time Budgets and Schedules Based on the Preceding Steps

Take out your big calendar again. Get a stack of 3x5 cards and the completed forms from the preceding steps.

As an example, look at Figure 3.7.

Use the calendar to establish a rough schedule. If you are radically changing procedures, carefully monitor the first few procedures to establish norms. If you are improving time use—as a result of becoming more aware of how time is actually being used—you may be able to shorten lead times. But don't plan on it until those new norms are habitual.

Wait until routines are debugged before tightening the schedule. For example, when companies move from manual to automated bookkeeping systems, most accountants suggest running two systems (old and new) for several months. You know the old system works; you hope the new system will.

Once the rough schedule is down on the calendar (goals, benchmarks along the way to getting to the goals), take the completed forms, any notes on how to change, alter, or otherwise improve work patterns, and a stack of 3x5 cards.

Figure 3.7

# Example of Calendar/Card Scheduling

## January 1987

A handwritten January 1987 calendar showing scheduled tasks.

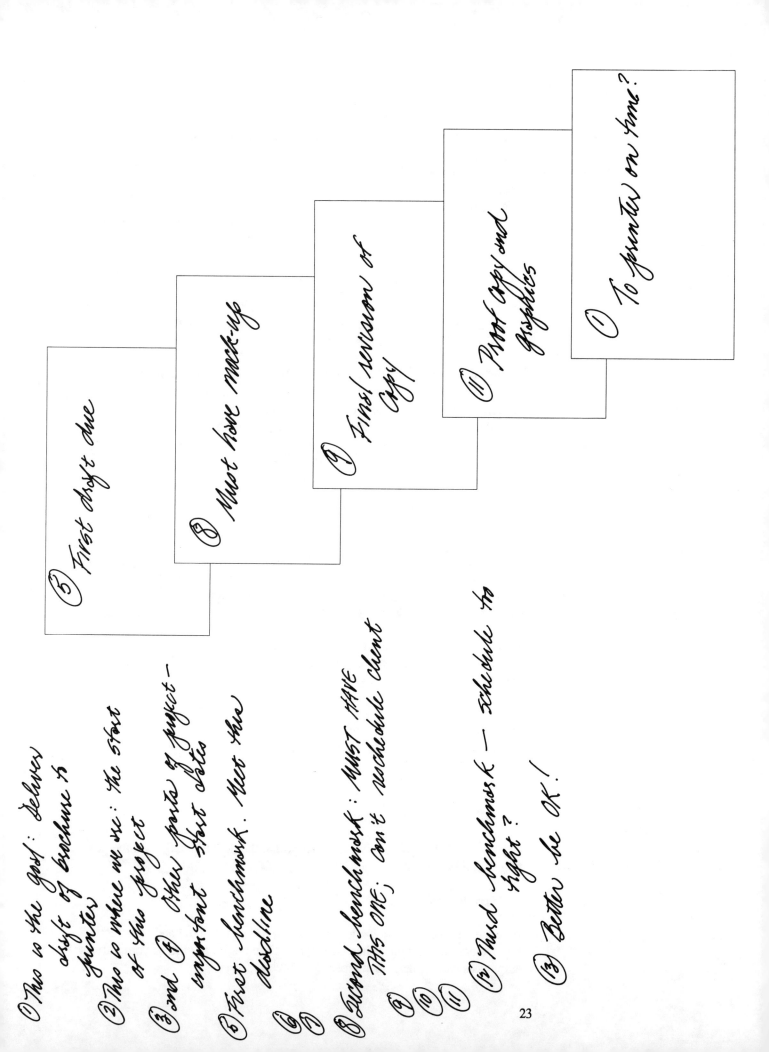

(1) This is the goal: deliver draft of brochure to printer

(2) This is where we are: the start of this project

(3) and (4) Other parts of project — important start dates

(5) First benchmark. Meet this deadline

(6)

(7)

(8) Second benchmark: MUST HAVE THIS ONE; can't reschedule client

(9)

(10)

(11)

(12) Third benchmark — schedule to fight? (tight?)

(13) Better be OK!

(5) First draft due

(8) Must have mock-up

(9) Final revision of copy

(11) Proof copy and graphics

(1) To printer on time?

23

List the tasks, one to each 3x5 card.

Make sure you include managerial tasks—not just machine and employee time.

You can now decide how time should be spent for the first week. You know what the week's goals are (and that reaching them helps you get to company objectives). You know who should be doing the specific tasks, when and where. You know how long these tasks should take (the norms) or at least have a good estimate from those closest to the actual tasks.

The remaining wrinkles in the schedule will come mostly from transportation, inspection, storage and decision. As you spread the 3x5s in a line from the first task to the last, be alert for possible snags and delays. This informal work flow analysis is a good source of ideas on improving work flow. Write these ideas down. The finest memory is not so firm as faded ink.

More improvements in the final schedule will come from returning to the sequence of 3x5s again and again. Keep track of potential danger spots and bottlenecks. But don't reschedule or reorganize workable work-flow patterns without compelling reasons—and the input and cooperation of your employees.


**Do You Still Need Another Employee?**

Match up the information you have assembled with the resources and people available.

For each employee, check again how his or her time is actually being used. Is there extra time available? When? Are the skills appropriate to the tasks? If all employees are working up to capacity, and there's slack time left, fine. Too tight a schedule leads to anger, frustration, and sloppy workmanship.

So does too loose a schedule. Better pay some overtime than have a bunch of bored, underemployed employees collecting weekly paychecks. No overtime indicates overstaffing.

Ask:
- [ ] What tasks need more time?
- [ ] Do a lot of jobs have to be done over? For better quality, do it right the first time.
- [ ] Are there new tasks to be done?
- [ ] Are sales increasing?
- [ ] Is the change temporary or permanent?

Lay out the 3x5s again. This time incorporate the new tasks. Should the position be full or part-time?

Still need that employee?

If yes, begin working on the job description (Chapter Four) and start recruiting. Otherwise, sit tight. When paying overtime begins to hurt, or your current employees call for help, then repeat the process.

# Chapter Four:
# What Are Job Descriptions For?

Job descriptions form the basis of personnel management.

Think of a director staging a play, or a baseball manager assembling a team. Your job is similar—in order to get the right kind of performance from your business, you have to staff it correctly and match the requirements of the job to the skills and abilities of your employees.

If you get the right players in the first place, your job is greatly simplified.

Get the wrong ones, though, and performance is going to suffer. Think of the baseball team: If you need a first baseman, you'd start by thinking of what the job consists of. Next, what skills and abilities does the position require? What are the most desirable characteristics of a first baseman? Among other things, sure hands and an ability to catch baseballs, and a proven ability to hit curve balls with power. Other preferred characteristics include height, left-handedness, and "coachability."

The same kind of process applies to staffing a small business. You don't have much room for error, so plan ahead. The Employee Planning Form (Figure 4.1) is a good starting point.

**Your employees are your best single source of information about operations in your business.**

## The Job Description Process

*Step One: Fill out Figure 4.1 for each position, actual or contemplated.* This will help you (and your employee) to better understand just what the job involves, how much time each task takes, and lay the basis for a realistic job description, time-use improvement, productivity gains, performance evaluations, and even legally helpful information. If your business is small enough, you may want to simply list everything—every single activity you can think of—on this form, and then arrange them into logical jobs.

In either case, first list as many activities as you can think of, then go back and estimate the amount of time each activity should take.

*Step Two: Review the preliminary Employee Planning Form with your employees.* They will spot omissions and errors, and will have helpful comments. Your employees are your best single source of information about operations in your business. Put their expertise to work for you.

Once the form has been reviewed and corrections made, put it aside for a day or two. Then return to it.

**Job descriptions make replacing an employee much simpler.**

*Step Three: Add up all the times.* You may find that the total is excessive. Maybe some of the jobs are done concurrently, or are not necessary, or can be scheduled better, or be done by someone else.

As you review the results so far, keep in mind your overall objectives: to improve your business, to create realistic job descriptions, and to make very sure that you don't add unnecessary employees. This is where the comments section is especially helpful—jot down the ideas as they come along so they don't get lost. Ask, ask again, and listen.

*Step Four: Begin the Job Description, Figure 4.2.* If you already have job descriptions for each position, now is the time to compare each job description with what is actually being done to make sure that you don't miss any important function.

Job descriptions make replacing an employee much simpler—the job requirements are available, so the search for a replacement can start quickly. And since jobs change, another reason to maintain up-to-date job descriptions is to make sure there is no serious dislocation between the job description and the real world.

For all jobs, ask:
- [ ] Is this job necessary?
- [ ] Can it be done by someone else?
- [ ] Can it be done somewhere else? In a better way? At a better time?
- [ ] Has this job/position been reviewed recently? When?

Seize every opportunity to question the need for each job slot. You can't afford to carry dead weight. If you aren't currently paying overtime now and again, worry. Lack of overtime always signifies overstaffing.

*Step Five: Start at the beginning of the Job Description Form.* What's the title of the new job? Who is preparing the form? When?

Now fill in the functions and times (use Figure 4.1, Employee Planning Form for each job). Add up the times—most employees don't want to work 80-hour weeks. If the job is unrealistic, change the job. It's a lot easier to change a job than to change a person.

As you fill in the functions, keep in mind what skills, formal training, licensing, aptitude and experience apply to the job. You can always relax standards to get the right person, or a person who would be ideal with a bit more training.

Skills and qualifications must be job-related to avoid legal problems. If you have any question at all about whether or not your hiring practices are legal, check with your lawyer.

Once you know what the specs are and what the job involves, the hardest part of writing the job description is over. Updating a job description in small companies may have to be done frequently until routines become established,

26

but it's easier than making the first version. Remember: For each job, you must list key functions and establish norms.

There's an important principle involved here: Everyone needs to know what they are responsible for, even if the responsibilities are only sketched in. You will use the job descriptions for evaluating personnel, for promotions and salary reviews, for improving your business operations.

Most of all, though, you will use them to communicate clearly with your employees, and to ensure that the duties and responsibilities of each job are understood.

*Step Six: Finish the job description.* Write a brief synopsis of the duties, note who the person reports to, and review and list the job specifications. For a highly regimented job the list of functions tends to be longer than for a job with considerable autonomy. Your duties include some vague ones: planning, motivating, innovating, while a custodial job might include sweeping the sidewalks, washing windows, changing lightbulbs, and stocking shelves.

The job description and list of job specifications in the example (Figure 4.3) were used in the advertisement for the position, as a way to clarify what the job involved to the applicants, and as a preliminary screening tool. Note that the job specifications clearly pertain to the position. All the basic questions an applicant might reasonably ask are addressed—salary, basic skills, and experience needed.

No job description is complete without noting that it is not an implied contract or job offer (for applicants), nor is it iron-clad and proof against change as circumstances warrant.

The sentences at the bottom of the job description are there for a purpose. If you create your own form, include them—they may save you legal headaches. "We reserve the right to change or revise duties and responsibilities as the need arises. This document is not a written or implied contract of employment."

You should use job descriptions for all current employees, especially if you haven't been using job descriptions as a management tool. "Current employees" includes you.

**No job description is complete without noting that it is not an implied contract or job offer (for applicants), nor is it iron-clad and proof against change as circumstances warrant.**

27

Figure 4.1

# Employee Planning Form

Position or Name: _Senior Editor / Marketing_    Date: _6/21_

| Task/Function | Estimated Time | Comments |
|---|---|---|
| 1. Monthly re-writes | 10 | Increase freelance |
| 2. Editorials, projects | 16 | staff on these? |
| 3. List maintenance | 6? | Delegate; can be streamlined |
| 4. Edit freelance work | 6 | Increase? |
| 5. Editors meeting (Fri) | 4 | Should be 2 hrs? |
| 6. Sales/administration | 4 | Give to SHW? |
| 7. Customer support | 8 | Big part of job - but can delegate? |
| 8. | | |
| 9. Visit clients | 10 | Varies: How can we change this? |
| 10. re:Ports — write, edit | 15 | Can these be improved? |
| 11. re:Ports — administration | 5 | More freelance? Or is budget too tight? |
| 12. | | |
| 13. | | |
| 14. | | |
| 15. | | |
| 16. | | |
| 17. | | |
| 18. | | |
| 19. | | |
| 20. | | |
| Total Time: | 84 | |

How can we save 40± hours, or do we need help here?

Figure 4.2

# Job Description

Position: _Editorial Assistant_

Date Prepared: _6/25_

By: _AB_

| Task/Function | Estimated Hours Per Week |
|---|---|
| 1. Customer support | 6-8 |
| 2. Monthly re-writes | 10-12 |
| 3. Editorials, projects | 6-8 |
| 4. Re: Posts editorial and graphic support | 5-10 |
| 5. Research for editorial staff | 5-10 |
| 6. List maintenance | 3 |
| 7. Phone: Sales | 4 |
| 8. | |
| 9. | |
| 10. | |
| Total Hours: | 39-55 |

Comments:

**Job Description:**

Assist in editing and rewriting raw copy following style guidelines. Assist with sales support and occasional direct sales efforts. Help with production and other duties of periodical publications. Other tasks as management may require.
Responsible to Senior Editor
Hours: Full-time (40/week) with some evening and weekend work. Light travel on occasion.
Salary: to $1,500/month

**Job Specifications:**

Proven writing and editing skills. Some sales and business experience desirable. Must be able to learn, work with minimal supervision. Must be articulate in order to communicate with professional clientele.

Figure 4.3

## Example of a Job Description

**Position:** Editorial Assistant.

**Salary:** to $1,500/month.

Assist in editing and rewriting raw copy following style guidelines. Assist with production and other duties (setting type, paste up, layout, etc.) for periodical publications. Help with direct sales and sales support on occasion.

**Hours:**

Full-time (40 hours/week). Some evening and weekend work. Light travel (2 days/month).

**Reports to:**

Senior Editor

**Job Specifications:**

1. Communication skills <u>must be proven</u>. This person must be able to:
   —write clearly and simply
   —edit raw copy
   —work with freelance writers and artists
   —communicate clearly with professional clientele
2. Aptitudes:
   —ability to master financial and business terminology
   —work to deadlines with minimal supervision
3. Education and experience should demonstrate required skills and aptitudes.

We reserve the right to change or revise duties and responsibilities as the need arises. This document is not a written or implied contract of employment.

# Chapter Five:
# How Do I Get Good Employees?

Two important questions to ask yourself about current employees:

☐ If I knew then what I know now, would I have hired the same people?
☐ How would I change my choices—if I could turn back the clock?

Finding the right person for a job can be very frustrating. One consequence is that we sometimes pay less attention to the hiring process than we should, settling for the first warm body that approaches the specifications for the job.

Finding the right person calls for having information about the applicants, from their application forms, interviews, tests, and reference checks. Armed with this information, you can discriminate between those persons you think will work and those persons you aren't so sure of.

You cannot legally discriminate on the basis of sex, religion, creed, national origin, handicaps, or age. But the law doesn't imply that you can't select the best applicant from those you interview, nor does it compel you to hire anyone if you don't find the right person.

Where do you find people with the right skills and attitudes? By hiring intelligently from a pool of qualified applicants. If you have only one candidate, you run an enormous risk—and limit your choices.

Start with the job description. While you may be tempted to alter it to fit an attractive candidate, keep in mind that the reason you developed a job description in the first place was because certain functions have to be performed. The job description will help whether you advertise the job inside your business (a shot at a promotion is a great morale builder) or advertise outside, either through a newspaper or an employment agency.

A policy of selecting the best person for the job makes good sense—and if you find that person inside your business, great. If not, that's OK too; by bringing in an outsider you also bring in fresh ideas and insights. A policy of always promoting from within is as stultifying as never promoting from within. Hire the best person available.

*Step One: Get a number of qualified applicants to select from.* This may seem impossible at times, especially in a crowded labor market, but there are at least a dozen sources. See Figure 5.1 for a display of their positive and negative points.

Recruiting is part of your job, and has some hidden pitfalls. Of the various ways to find a pool of qualified applicants (the least expensive in the long run) is the most costly up front: specialized employment agencies for the most

**If you have only one candidate, you run an enormous risk—and limit your choices.**

skilled and/or important positions, followed by other employment agencies (including government agencies).

The smaller the company, the more nettlesome recruiting and interviewing is. A newspaper ad may appear to be an inexpensive way to go, until you spend a lot of time interviewing unqualified people. Develop a good working relationship with local agencies, including temporary agencies. Their job is recruiting, interviewing, and evaluating potential employees, and it stands to reason that they'll do a better job than most of us.

As an example, an ad based on the example (Figure 4.2) was placed in two metropolitan papers on successive Sundays. It drew more than 300 responses the first week. The time it took to respond to that flood of applicants—many well qualified—posed a major problem, as well as a considerable investment. The person who was finally hired, incidentally, never saw the ad. She was referred to us by a friend.

Recruit. Your advertisement—whether internal (bulletin board or direct communication with your employees) or external (employment agencies, institutions, newspapers, or trade bulletins) should be based on the job description you have carefully drawn up.

Figure 5.1

# Sources of Applicants

| Source | Advantages/ Disadvantages | Comments |
|---|---|---|
| 1. Current employees | You know their strengths and weaknesses. Promoting from within provides a chance for them to grow. But look out for favoritism, lack of new ways of doing things, and promoting an unqualified but senior person. | You must consider current employees first, for the sake of employee morale. |
| 2. Former employees | Same as above. | Consider retired workers for part-time work. |
| 3. Employee referrals | Recruitment costs are low, and these people can easily fit into your work force. But watch out for nepotism and formation of cliques. Lowered morale can follow if referral is not hired. | Stress that you will hire the best, most qualified candidate. |
| 4. Advertising | Your ad can reach a large number of people, and can aim at a target group via specific media. But you may get too many unqualified applicants. | Make your ad specific, and base it on the job description to avoid attracting weak candidates. |
| 5. Schools, colleges, etc. | Recruitment costs are low, and the school may screen candidates for you. Trade-off: enthusiasm for experience. | Many schools have active placement services. Make yourself known to them. |
| 6. Private employment agencies | These agencies will work for you, and will interview and screen candidates for you. But they are the most expensive short-term alternative. | The best solution for hard-to-fill jobs. Long-term, the least expensive alternative. |

*(continued on next page)*

Figure 5.1
*(continued from previous page)*

| Source | Advantages/ Disadvantages | Comments |
|---|---|---|
| 7. Public employment agencies | These agencies don't charge, and they provide excellent testing, job analysis, and indexing services. They will work with you and for you if they know your needs. But they may send unqualified or unmotivated applicants. | Get to know the local agency employees. |
| 8. Handicapped workers | These people are highly motivated, and tend to have low absenteeism. Service agencies will often help train them. But you may have insurance and facility access problems. | Involve present employees to help overcome their resistance. |
| 9. Professional societies | These societies have low or no fees, but their resources are limited. | Good source of professionals or managers. |
| 10. Labor unions | Unions have no fees and may provide a number of qualified applicants. But they may not send you their best applicants. | Good for skilled craft positions, e.g., electricians. |
| 11. Walk-ins | Their recruitment doesn't cost you anything, and they are interested in working for you. But they are an unstable source. | Make a file of these people's skills for future reference. |
| 12. Friends and relations | They know and like you, and may know the company well. But they may expect special treatment. | Ever fire a friend? However, they may be the only source in a startup or marginal business. |
| 13. Other businesses | No cost, may be a good source of candidates. But: Raiding another business will backfire. | Call and ask. |
| 14. Chamber of Commerce | No cost; may have knowledge of qualified administrative, sales, or managerial people new to your area. | Worth calling. |

The recruiting objective is simple: Get as many qualified applicants as you can. If you send a letter with the job description, salary range information and a notice of when and how to reach you to the sources listed on pages 33 and 34 (including those you have to pay—agencies, newspapers, etc.), you increase your chances of making a good selection.

Since the cost of a bad hire is so large—look at the disruption and bad feelings alone if wasted time and salary don't make the point clearly enough—the apparent cost of using an employment agency is less than it appears. Depending on the job, the employment agency charge will range from 10% to 30% or more of the employee's first year's salary.

Begin your search inside your business. While you may not find the right person, the attention and possibility of a promotion is a morale booster. If training could make an employee ready for a promotion, consider it carefully. (See Chapter Eight for more on internal promotions.)

*Step Two: Have all applicants fill out an application blank.* A legal application form is provided (Figure 5.2: Employee Application Form) in Appendix One. You may want to get a more specialized form—ask an employment agency. If you want to be doubly sure that it is legal, check with your lawyer. The information the application form provides helps you make a sensible hiring decision. (Figure 5.2 has been checked by an attorney to make sure it won't get you into legal hot water.)

*Step Three: Cull the applicants.* You want to choose the best applicant from a number of qualified applicants, but unless you're a masochist, you don't want to interview everyone remotely interested in the job.

Look for two kinds of information: Can the applicant do the job? Will the applicant do the job?

Those applicants who don't meet the job specs may be fine for another job. File their applications for future reference. Usually it's easy to weed out applicants, such as those who want more money than the job is worth. (See Chapter Six for setting pay scales.)

Now go through the applications of those who apparently meet the job requirements. These are the ones to interview. If the number is unwieldy, look for other ways to sort them out. Look for gaps in their applications, and seek clarification.

After you've weeded out as many as possible, check the references of those remaining. If you don't have three candidates left, recruit some more—you owe yourself a good selection.

Reference checks are tricky. An applicant who is refused a job on the basis of a reference is legally entitled to a copy of the reference, so many people won't give you adverse information. This puts the person giving the reference in an awkward spot—so be careful.

**Look for two kinds of information: Can the applicant do the job? Will the applicant do the job?**

**Your aim is to get the reference to talk.**

"He was an average or below average worker" is an opinion, not defensible. Don't use it. Subjective references unsupported by facts are useless.

When checking references, look for facts: dates of graduation, employment dates, and other defendable information. Some questions that can help you make a decision are:

"Can-Do" Questions:
1. Did he/she work for you as a _____?
2. Did he/she perform to your satisfaction?
3. What did he/she do well?
4. What did he/she do poorly?
5. Would you rehire him/her?
6. Why or why not?

"Will-Do" Questions:
1. He/she says he/she left your company because _____. Could you tell me more about that?
2. Would you rate his or her attendance as average, below average, or above average?
3. Did he/she get along well with customers and fellow workers?
4. Did he/she respond well to close supervision on the job?

Your aim is to get the reference to talk. You can always ask them to comment further, but don't be surprised, given the current legal mood, if some references choose not to comment. (And "I'd rather not comment on that" is a particularly revealing comment!)

Since the reason you hire Person A rather than Person B is that you think A is better matched to the job requirements, you won't want to dwell on adverse references anyway.

On a more positive note, sometimes you will receive such a glowing reference that the essentially negative function of reference checking is overlooked. If you have an applicant who is heartily endorsed by more than one reference, you may have a gem. Check anyway; the rule on references is L.I.A.R.—Look Into All References.

Take the applications of those you don't wish to consider further, let them know that you want to keep their applications on hand against a future recruitment, and proceed to interview the remaining applicants.

Figure 5.3
# Interviewer's Guidelines

## I. Define the interview's purpose beforehand:
☐ Determine ability to do the job.

☐ Determine willingness to do the job.

## II. Procedure:
☐ Review application, check references before the interview.

☐ Relax applicant.

☐ Describe the job as thoroughly as possible.

☐ Give applicant a copy of the job description.

☐ Ask questions about prior employment: dates, duties, locations.

☐ Then ask: likes, dislikes, why he or she left the jobs, what kinds of supervision and working conditions are preferred.

☐ Then ask about the applicant's expectations for the job. Look for fits and mismatches with the realities of the job (money, hours, opportunities for growth and advancement, job security and so on).

☐ *After eliciting the applicant's expectations:* give information about policies, working conditions, advantages of working for your company, your own expectations for the prospective employee. If you were to present this information sooner, you'd get back an echo: what the applicant thinks you want to hear.

☐ Give the applicant your time frame for making the hiring decision.

☐ *Do not hire on the spot.* Check references further; get results of physical and skill tests if indicated.

## III. Follow-up:
☐ After applicant leaves: jot down impressions, questions you wished you had asked, thoughts for following up in a further interview. Use Figure 5.6: Selection Summary Sheet.

☐ If you decide not to hire the applicant, then tell him/her, explaining only that the applicant who best matched the requirements of the job was hired. The reason to choose one candidate over another is always that the one hired was better matched to the job requirements, even if part of the reason was an adverse reference.

*Step Four: Interview the top candidates.* This may take two steps: If a test (either skills, or physical, or both) is needed, have all the remaining applicants take it. The actual interview is the least accurate step of the selection process, if only because most of us don't interview a lot, don't have the necessary skills for it, tend to have biases of which we are unaware, and find the process a bit embarrassing. Ever interview someone and find that you spend most of the time talking about your business, the job, and how important it is—and not let the applicant talk? It happens all the time.

Open questions—those that can't be answered with a simple yes or no— elicit the most information. Plan for the interview, ask the questions, and listen to the response.

---

Figure 5.4
**Sample Interview Questions**

You want to get the applicant to talk—and provide as much "can do" and "will do" information as you need. Jot down questions before the interview, and you will learn more than you would in an unstructured interview.

- ☐ Are you familiar with _____ (process or machine)?
- ☐ How would you handle an enraged customer?
- ☐ What would you do if _____?
- ☐ What did you like (dislike) about the previous job? School?
- ☐ Of all the supervisors (teachers) you've had, describe the one you liked best. Describe the one you liked least.
- ☐ How much pay do you expect for this kind of work?
- ☐ What type of work do you expect to be doing in two years? Five years?
- ☐ If you could pick any job in the world, what would you pick? Why?
- ☐ What's most important to you about a job?
- ☐ If we asked your previous boss about your job performance, what do you think he/she would say?
- ☐ What do you believe are your strong points? Your weak points?
- ☐ To any response: Ask, "Why?"

And so forth. Open questions get the applicant talking. Listening helps you make a better decision. You can always ask for more detail.

---

There are questions you may not legally ask. Figure 5.5 outlines the boundaries. If in doubt, do not ask the question.

Figure 5.5
**Screening Practices and the Law**

Questions you may wish to ask may put you on questionable legal ground.

| | **You May:** | **You May Not:** |
|---|---|---|
| Name | Ask for the name (and maiden name) of an applicant, and if he/she was a former employee under another name. | Inquire into the national or religious origin of the name, or ask if it was changed. |
| Address | Ask for the current address and length of residence. | Ask for a past foreign address. |
| Age, Place of Birth | | Ask the applicant's age or date of birth, or require birth certificate, naturalization, or baptismal papers. |
| Religion | | Question the applicant's religion, religious beliefs, parish, names of clergy, or religious holidays observed. |
| Race or Color | | Ask questions relating directly to race or color. |
| Marital Status | Determine if applicant is married, single, divorced or widowed. | |
| Number and Age of Children | Ask the number of dependents. Ask whether they are in school. | Ask age of children or childcare arrangements. |
| Citizenship | Inquire if applicant is a US citizen. If an alien, you may determine if the applicant has permission to remain in the country and has a work permit. | Inquire whether the applicant's spouse or parents are native born or naturalized, or request dates of naturalization or application papers. |
| Education | Obtain names of schools, level of education and graduation dates. | Establish a non-job related educational requirement, or ask the racial, national, or religious affiliation of schools attended. |

*(continued on next page)*

Figure 5.5
*(continued from previous page)*

|  | You May: | You May Not: |
|---|---|---|
| **Military Service** | Inquire into the applicant's military background, skills learned, and rank attained. | Determine type of discharge, request discharge papers or inquire into the applicant's foreign military service. |
| **Organizations** | Inquire into organizations of which the applicant is a member, providing the organization does not reveal religion, race, color or national origin of its members. You may ask what offices the applicant held. | Request the names of the organizations. |
| **Health-Related** | Determine height, weight, and handicap data. | Set minimum or maximum height, weight, or other physical requirements for the job. |

Once you have interviewed all of the applicants, make your decision. To prevent the "last interviewed, first hired" syndrome, use Figure 5.6: Selection Summary Sheet, to keep all of the applicants' strong and weak points in mind.

Figure 5.6
**Selection Summary Sheet**

Date: _7/9/86_
Interviewer: _JEK_

Position: _Editorial Assistant_
Candidate's Name: _DISGUISED_

Comments:

**"Can Do" Factors:**

Needs some training — not much experience (6 months of editing college paper). Gets things done on time (no "incompletes" on transcripts — is this good or bad?)

**"Will Do" Factors:**

High enthusiasm — offered to work for $0 to prove herself, or do intern for the summer. Likes to be self-directed.

1. Stability: Good track record — summer and campus jobs.
2. Need for job: New graduate with loans to pay; need to make a living.
3. Attitude towards supervision: Enjoys research — self-directed?
4. Ability to work with others: (?)
5. Skills and experience: College level writing which can be improved. Some word processing — limited experience in this field but
6. Attitude towards training: Eager to learn.
7. Expectations about job: Lots of challenge, responsibility — may want promotion too soon? ENTHUSIASTIC.
8. Other factors (specify): Energetic; enthusiastic
Eager for responsibility
Might want to try a big city job as soon as she has some experience to bargain with.

---

Use Figure 5.6 only as a jog to your memory. It is not a rating form, and if used as shown in the example, it will be legally justifiable. A rating system that applies different weights to different job factors can be a problem: How do you justify a rating of seven over a rating of eight for "expectations about job?"

Once you make your decision, let the other candidates know that a candidate you think is better matched to the job has been hired, and ask if they would be interested in having their name kept on file for further job openings. If you have followed the steps indicated in the preceding chapters, most will say, "please do,"—and you will build a pool of qualified, interested applicants for future job openings.

There is no mechanical selection process—but if you have had consistently high turnover or a record of making poor personnel choices, or if you are unsure, do what you'd do with a legal or medical problem. Get professional help.

# Chapter Six:
# What About Pay and Fringe Benefits?

You want to pay well enough to attract and retain competent employees, but not more than you have to. At the same time, you want to be sure to be fair—equal pay for equal work makes good business and legal sense. If your employees think you are unfair or play favorites, you'll have a severe morale problem to deal with.

As for your own compensation, the IRS has set some limits. If you are taking what they consider to be an excessive salary, they'll allot part of your compensation to dividends and tax you accordingly. Ask you accountant whether your salary could be considered excessive. If it is tied to company performance, and is backed up with records and corporate minutes, you'll probably be OK—but better be safe.

Compensation has two parts: pay, whether salary or wages, and benefits.

*Step One: Establish salary and wage levels.* Look for current going rates. You can get reasonably up-to-date lists of regional averages, broken down by job, from the Department of Labor's Bureau of Labor Statistics or from state employment agencies. You can also get a close approximation by watching newspaper want ads, asking other business owners, and sometimes by calling local business schools. If you have established a good relationship with local employment agencies, they'll provide the best salary information of all—they have to be very up-to-date to do their job.

Once you know what the average salaries are for the job (as described in the job description), establish a range ±10%. You won't be far wrong if you offer the low end to an inexperienced applicant, and reserve the higher end for either bargaining or providing room for salary growth that won't put your pay scales out of balance.

If the going rate for a secretary in your area is $6.00 an hour, set your range at $5.40 to $6.60. That allows you to get a competent secretary, have some room for a raise if warranted, and replace him or her if necessary. Someone else may offer a lot more money than you think the job is worth.

You can expect some employees to push for more wages, and even quit (or threaten to) if you don't meet their demands. That's to be expected. If you have a ±10% range, you will at least buy some time. At some point you have to say no, the job is worth only so much money, not a nickel more. Money—pay—is a peculiar subject. Money means different things to different people.

**Recognition is fine, but money is still the most easily understood incentive.**

If you can, establish a tie between your profits and the employee's contributions to the company. The clearest link: commission on sales beyond a pre-set quota. Pure commission salespeople are hard to find, and most studies show that a salary plus commission results in higher long-term profits at a lower cost than a straight commission. Straight commission compensation may temporarily increase sales—but if customer service after the sale is important, this form of compensation could jeopardize profits.

Suggestion programs are a good example of a direct tie between contribution and reward. All of your employees have ideas that can help make your business more profitable, and a formal plan makes it clear that you listen to their ideas. Figure 6.1 on the next page is a suggestion form you can adapt to suit your purposes. (No program will work if you don't listen to the employees—if they think it's just a sham, a suggestion program is counterproductive.)

Establish award policies, and post them. Make sure you include a review procedure, no matter how simple, to arbitrate possible disputes.

The recognition factor is vital to this kind of program, so keep a public list of who submits ideas, how many, and how many have been accepted. Involve the employees as far as you can in evaluating suggestions—the hands-on process cements the recognition factor.

Recognition is fine, but money is still the most easily understood incentive. Tie the actual amounts to recognizing the employee's contribution to the company whenever possible. If you provide small cash rewards for suggestions, productivity improvements, cost-saving ideas and so on, your employees have an added incentive and know that you notice their contributions to the business' success.

Group awards are a different matter. If an improvement in productivity is made, it may not be attributable to an individual but really be a group function. Fine; make the award to the group.

Make the awards quickly. Don't wait until year-end, when the link between contribution reward is dimmed by time. Make it fast, make it public, and make it valuable to the business as well as the employee.

Figure 6.1
**Suggestion Form**

---

Instructions: Write your suggestions clearly, indicating what should be done, why, and how you think it will help the business. If you need more space, or if you need a sketch to make your idea clear, attach extra sheets of paper. All suggestions submitted will be reviewed, and we will keep you informed of the progress of your idea. Thanks.

From: _____          Date: _____

My suggestion is:


It should accomplish:


It will take the following (people, equipment, time, money):

_____

Action Taken:

Discussed with Employee(s) by _____    Date: _____

---

*Step Two: What benefits do you offer?* Fringe benefits—the other part of the compensation package—amount, on average, to 30% of salary. While you may not be able to compete with big companies on some fringe benefits, you can make sure that your employees know what benefits they are receiving, offer them some non-cash (and non-traditional) benefits that a bigger company cannot, and, most important of all, be able to respond to their needs.

Employee concerns include:
☐   Retirement, financial planning, tax minimization programs
☐   Health care and health insurance
☐   Life and disability (income replacement) insurance
☐   Growth, recognition, achievement, and participation opportunities
☐   Security for their family
☐   Job security

As you put together the compensation package, your concerns include:
☐   Attracting and keeping good employees
☐   Motivating and training personnel
☐   Being fair to all employees
☐   Recognizing employee performance
☐   Protecting employees (insurance, job security)
☐   Providing retirement income
☐   Providing opportunities to build capital

45

**You have a great deal of flexibility in designing your benefit package— but with this flexibility, there's a lot of red tape. Hence the need for legal and tax counsel.**

Look at Figure 6.2: A List of Possible Fringe Benefits. It may spark some ideas on structuring a benefit plan that helps both you and your employees. Get tax and legal counsel to make sure that you don't create future problems. This is especially important for benefits that apply to you as the owner but not to employees. Also, review retirement programs and insurance.

As you review the list in Figure 6.2, ask:
- [ ] Would this be attractive to my employees?
- [ ] How much will it cost? (Now and later.)
- [ ] What are the budget limitations?
- [ ] Is the plan legal?
- [ ] Is the plan tax wise?
- [ ] What is the purpose of the plan?
- [ ] Does it fit the needs of my employees?
- [ ] How extensive should it be? Who will be covered?
- [ ] What will the eligibility requirements be?
- [ ] Should the employees contribute?

You have a great deal of flexibility in designing your benefit package—but with this flexibility, there's a lot of red tape. Hence the need for legal and tax counsel. For example, you can establish eligibility requirements of six months employment before joining a medical insurance plan—but that requirement has to apply to everybody, not just a particular employee. Vendors will explain the ins and outs of eligibility requirements, but it pays to have your attorney make sure that you are indeed legal.

Many small companies ask their employees to share some of the costs of insurance programs, especially health and disability insurance. Membership in a group plan can offer substantial savings to both employer and employee. Limit your premium payments—pay (for example) 50% of the premium, and have the employee pay the rest. Or pay the entire premium this year, but pass on the inevitable premium increases to the employees. They get top coverage; you get protected against premium inflation.

Figure 6.2
# A List of Possible Fringe Benefits

**Legally Required:** Check with your lawyer and accountant for details. The particulars change, and you want to protect yourself.
- ☐ Social Security (FICA)
- ☐ Workers Compensation insurance
- ☐ Federal Unemployment insurance (FUTA)
- ☐ Continuation of medical insurance (employers with 20 or more employees)
- ☐ In some states, state unemployment insurance
- ☐ In some states, employee disability insurance
- ☐ Pay while on jury duty, military reserve
- ☐ Parental and medical leaves may become mandatory: Check with your lawyer

**Direct Cash Benefits:** These optional benefits cost you cash.
- ☐ Medical expense benefits
- ☐ Life, accident and health insurance
- ☐ Membership in HMOs (Health Maintenance Organizations)
- ☐ Disability income insurance
- ☐ Retirement plans (see Chapter Eleven)
- ☐ Profit sharing
- ☐ Dental care, prescription drug, vision care, group life plans
- ☐ Legal services

**Indirect Cash Benefits:** Costly, valuable, and often overlooked as benefits because they are so common.
- ☐ Paid holidays
- ☐ Paid vacations
- ☐ Paid sick leave
- ☐ Paid time off: funeral, "mental health" or personal days, birthdays, dental or medical appointments, attendance at school events
- ☐ Free lunch, uniform, transportation
- ☐ Educational benefits
- ☐ Recreation services (health club membership, for example)
- ☐ Company trips, parties, celebrations

**Noncash Benefits:** While these have costs attached, they are hard to put figures to.
- ☐ Flexible time schedules
- ☐ Job sharing
- ☐ Coffee breaks
- ☐ Childcare
- ☐ Release time
- ☐ Sabbaticals, unpaid time off (for long trips, for example)
- ☐ Company teams
- ☐ Personal use of company equipment, facilities
- ☐ Access to company legal and accounting help

**Small Companies' Greatest Benefits:** You have wide flexibility, close communication with your employees, and more latitude than a big company in matching business and employee personal needs.

**You have wide flexibility, close communication with your employees, and more latitude than a big company in matching business and employee personal needs.**

You can probably add to the list—your imagination is the only barrier. As an example of an unusual fringe benefit, Upstart Publishing allows employees to bring their dogs to the office (provided the dogs are well trained).

*Step Three: Make employees aware of the value of the benefits.* Fringe benefits are expensive. Once you know what benefits you offer (including the legally mandated benefits), make sure that you communicate that value to your employees.

One way to do this is on the paycheck—but this has the drawback of not showing some of the less obvious but most valuable benefits that your business can offer. Some insurance companies provide brochures detailing the value of their services to your employees.

We recommend using Figure 6.3: Total Compensation, to keep your employees aware of their total compensation. Fill it out and distribute it once a quarter, when you have quarterly tax statements to provide base information.

Figure 6.3
**Total Compensation**

Name of Employee: *Foy*        Date: *6/1/86*

**During the past quarter, your total compensation included:**

Salary/Wages for quarter:     $ *3,600.00*

Social Security paid by company:     $ *257.40*

Workers Compensation premium:     $ *72.00*

Unemployment tax paid:     $ *126.00*

Other federal, state, local premiums:     $ *27.00*

Health, Accident and Life Insurance:     $ *558.00*

Educational benefits:     $ *125.00*

Total:     $ *4,765.40*   (*32% of base*)

**Other benefits:**
Number of paid vacation days:     *0*

Number of paid holidays:     *4*

Number of paid sick days:     *2*

Number of paid personal days:     *1*

Other benefits (specify):     *Advance on salary to meet tuition date*

Adapt Figure 6.3 to the benefits you offer—add profit sharing, for example, or company contribution to pension plan or free childcare if appropriate. The total amount per employee may well give you a jolt—the first time. It will be more than you expect.

That's one reason it's so important to communicate it to your employees.

A way to communicate informal benefits should be used. Weekly meetings are a good time—take advantage of the communicaton potential. It's your best way to keep good employees.

# Chapter Seven:
# How Do I Get a New Employee Up to Speed?

The first day on a new job is always confusing—especially for a new employee, although many of the same concerns apply to a newly promoted person who must learn new ways of dealing with other employees.

Orientation and training go together. Make orientation the first part of training, and you prevent a lot of stress. All of your employees benefit from orientation—working a new person into the group and changing work patterns is not easy.

There are many questions employees forget to ask: What about changes in insurance programs, pensions, vacation or release time policies, fringe benefits? Orientation is a good time to share company goals with all your employees—especially if goals have changed or are going to change.

Figure 7.1, First Day Orientation Form, will help cover three broad areas when orientating a new employee:
- ☐ Company rules and policies
- ☐ Introduction to the people who will be working with or supervising the new employee
- ☐ The physical plant and safety rules.

Set a time for a review with the employee at the end of his/her first week on the job. You want to answer his/her questions, improve the orientation process, and make sure the new employee is settling in well.

Review the job description with the employee and make sure he or she knows what their responsibilities are. As you review the job description, set performance goals with the employee—then, when it's time for review and evaluation of performance you'll have a good agenda to work from.

A new employee should receive an orientation at the end of the first week. Adjusting to the new work environment and fitting into a different group of co-workers is difficult and confusing, so you want to make the transition as smooth as possible. When you review the first week, let the employee ask questions. You may have to do some prompting, since he or she won't necessarily know what to ask.

> **Orientation and training go together. Make orientation the first part of training, and you prevent a lot of stress.**

**By making training available early, you also make a statement: This company wants its employees to grow.**

Once the employee has had a chance to get used to the way your business operates, training to sharpen his or her skills may be indicated. One week should give a clue to the employee's needs, especially if you ask the employee what kind of added skills are needed to do the job.

Training provides a lot for an employee: a sense of growth and achievement, knowledge that management (you) is interested in improving his or her skills, and recognition of his or her potential to advance. By making training available early, you also make a statement: This company wants its employees to grow.

You have to look ahead to the needs of your business—so don't confine training to new hires or to problem employees. One of the biggest selling points for a small business is a reputation for helping employees to grow into more responsible positions. This significantly reduces turnover and personnel costs; few people like to stick with a dead-end job. Those who do aren't the kind of employees you want.

To promote from within, you have to have well-qualified personnel. That calls for serious training efforts.

What kinds of training are appropriate? It depends on your work force, their skills and interests, your plans, and the needs your business faces in the future. As with other aspects of management, a little planning goes a long way. Comparing job descriptions to the people available is one part of the planning process. Another is to ask:

1. What skills will these jobs demand in the future?
2. What skills are getting rusty, outmoded, obsolete—and how can they be replaced, sharpened, upgraded?
3. How about interpersonal skills, sales training, pre-retirement training, and other less tangible training needs?

Most training efforts concentrate on job-related skills, but non-job-related training pays big morale dividends. Even if the skill an employee wants to pick up seems useless, think of it this way: An employee willing to put time and effort into learning new skills is apt to be more valuable over the long run than an employee content with present skill levels.

52

Figure 7.1

# First Day Orientation Form

Employee name: _____

Position: _____

Date hired: _____ Date started: _____

Person responsible for orientation: _____

Date for review: _____

Employee file opened by: _____ Date: _____

Check box for each item completed.
- ☐ Application received and filed?
- ☐ References checked?
- ☐ Performance test results evaluated and filed?
- ☐ Date set for evaluation reports: _____ By: _____
- ☐ W4 and Insurance forms given to employee?
- ☐ Employment Eligibility Verification (Form I-9) given to employee?

**Orientation**
First Day:
- ☐ Welcome
- ☐ Show coatroom, coffee machine, bathroom, other amenities
- ☐ Explain safety regulations
- ☐ Review: working hours, lunch hours, coffee breaks, parking
- ☐ Review job description
- ☐ Describe work
- ☐ Introduce to coworkers
- ☐ Introduce to supervisor
- ☐ Show operation
- ☐ Observe employee perform
- ☐ Review safety rules with employee
- ☐ Let employee know when you are available
- ☐ Check progress at end of first day; ask questions

Figure 7.2

# First Week Orientation Form

Employee name: _____

Position: _____

Reviewed by: _____

Date: _____

Date for next review: _____

At the end of the employee's first week, a brief interview to clarify rules and answer questions about the business is important. Try to get the employee to talk as much as possible—the first week establishes lasting impressions for both of you.

Check off each item after it is discussed.

- ☐  Review job description with employee

- ☐  Review progress

- ☐  Discuss training needs

- ☐  Set performance goals with employee

- ☐  Write down performance goals; give copy to employee

- ☐  Review pay procedures

- ☐  Review benefits (see Figure 6.3)

- ☐  Set date for next review

**Training Needs**

Comments: _____

_____

_____

_____

Prepared by: _____

Figure 7.3

# Training Alternatives

| Training Method | Pros | Cons |
|---|---|---|
| 1. On the job | Low cost, direct benefit to company, can be controlled | Ties up other productive workers, machinery; need skilled teacher |
| 2. Conference or coaching | Can be tailored to individual, low cost, flexible | Ties up supervisor, can lead to unrealistic hopes if not carefully monitored |
| 3. Apprentice | Highly focused, easy to measure progress, some government programs available | High cost of paying apprentice; time taken away from skilled workers |
| 4. Classroom | Allows many people to be taught at once, cost-effective for groups | Limited interaction, cost of released time and teacher may be excessive; retention lower than hands on |
| 5. Programmed instruction | Low cost, portable, very good for some technical material | Hard to find for specific skills; too costly to develop in-house |
| 6. Rotational: Let employees trade jobs | Good for morale, tests employees in various capacities | Apt to slow down productivity, requires a large number of people and jobs for effective use; may raise hopes too far |
| 7. Projects and committees | Low cost, wide exposure to management, broad range of possible tasks | Time consuming; can be dominated by wrong people; hard on timid people; difficult to measure. |
| 8. In-house training | Accurately pinpoint needs and skills; easy to measure and control | High cost tends to inflate fixed training costs, unless closely managed; may need professional help. |
| 9. Professional clubs, trade and business associations | Exposure to new ideas and new techniques; wide range of programs; good for trade relations | May lead to heavy recruitment of your best people; uneven quality of programs; cost may exceed benefits |
| 10. Role playing or management games | Can help air views, feelings, alleviate internal problems; can help you understand your own management style | Can degenerate into expensive game; low carryover into work situation |

**Training is important in preparing employees for promotion, increasing the value of your business, and helping problem employees become more effective.**

Training is important in preparing employees for promotion, increasing the value of your business, and helping problem employees become more effective. It is too valuable a tool to ignore.

How do you recognize a need for training? In part by observing employees on the job, in part by keeping track of productivity and progress toward your company's goals. Training can:

- ☐ Reduce turnover
- ☐ Reduce accidents
- ☐ Speed up growth
- ☐ Improve morale
- ☐ Reduce waste
- ☐ Improve output

Which training method should you use? It depends. The circumstances of your business and the training needs you identify will help you make this decision. Use Figure 7.4 to determine what those needs are.

OJT (On-the-job training) is the most common training technique. Decide what is to be taught, who is to teach it, and what results you are looking for. If you do the training, you benefit by getting to know the employee better, gaining a clearer understanding of the process or skill being taught, and perhaps finding ways to improve the operation.

In OJT the employee is shown, step by step, how a process is performed. Then the employee performs the operation, under close supervision, until it is done right. Finally, evaluate the performance, offer suggestions for improvement if needed, and jointly set some goals to be reviewed at a later date.

This can take enormous amounts of time—and your time is valuable. On the other hand, it can be done over time, in odd moments, and is the easiest mode of training to master.

Apprentice programs link the new employee to a skilled employee, who teaches the skills and tricks of the trade. A sales trainee, for example, may start out in the stock room to gain familiarity with the products you sell, then go out on the road a few times to observe an experienced salesperson in action, then make presentations under the observation of the experienced salesperson, and finally make calls on his or her own. This step-by-step process works if you can afford the time.

Job rotation lets employees try out other jobs in the business. This gives you a flexible work force, is excellent for morale because people don't get tracked into one slot, and makes it easier to replace key employees. The drawback is lower productivity—but the pluses of a well-rounded work force which understands many different jobs may be worth the cost. You can introduce job rotation in a limited way: a few hours a week. Your employees will look at job rotation as a fringe benefit.

The other forms of training in Figure 7.3 all have their place, though they are less common in smaller businesses. Still, with the competition for skilled and willing workers on the rise in most areas, consider using these other forms of training. People like to learn. Give your employees the opportunity and encouragement, and all of you will benefit.

**People like to learn. Give your employees the opportunity and encouragement, and all of you will benefit.**

---

Figure 7.4
## Employee Training Needs

Name of employee: *F O's*                    Date: *7/10/86*

Reviewed with employee:  ☑ Yes   ☐ No       By: *AB*

Improvements suggested in these areas:

1. *Time use — starts and stops jobs too often. Needs to follow through to end.*

2. *Use of computer for repetitive work.*

3.

4.

5.

Suggested solutions:

1. *Coaching: Ask JEK to assist.*

2. *OJT: AB to set some tasks with deadlines, and monitor progress. Also some classwork — check with local university.*

3.

4.

5.

Training scheduled to start:

1. *ASAP*

2. *Started this AM. FO's to check with UNH and respond to me by next week.*

3.

4.

5.

Copy to employee. Original to file.

---

# Chapter Eight:
# How Can I Keep Good Employees?

Keeping good employees is no accident.

*First, you have to hire well.* Follow some logical steps. Determine the job need, write a job description, recruit and select from a number of qualified applicants, orientate and train new (and newly promoted) employees. Pay them adequately.

*Second, treat your employees well.* The basic rule of personnel management is simple: Do unto others as you would have others do unto you. Keep in mind what you would want in a job:

- ☐ Fair wages
- ☐ Job security
- ☐ Agreeable working conditions: reasonable hours, safe, clean and well-lit work space, a pleasant environment
- ☐ A sense of improving your talents, worth, and status
- ☐ A sense of contribution to the company and the community
- ☐ Respect for and from management

These are satisfiers. All must be maintained to prevent employee dissatisfaction.

*Third, recognize that you don't motivate employees.* Employees motivate themselves. All you can do is destroy their motivation—unless you make it a careful policy to provide more than the satisfiers mentioned above.

Your employees are adults. Treat them accordingly. The more autonomy you encourage, the more control they have over their work and the better they will perform for you.

There are exceptions. That's why personnel management is necessary. You have to set rules and standards, and help employees set objectives that contribute to the achievement of your company goals. Performance evaluations (see Chapter Nine) serve a number of needs, not the least of which is to fairly reward those who are making progress and provide guidance for those who are not.

This doesn't mean that you become a patsy for lazy or careless workers. You have to make a profit to stay in business (or meet your budget if your organization is non-profit). Keeping non-productive employees on staff is a quick way to destroy everyone's job. You lose the respect of good employees by setting double standards for unproductive employees—a violation of the

**The more autonomy you encourage, the more control your employees have over their work and the better they will perform for you.**

**Nobody likes to toil without being recognized—if their work is worth their hire, they want it to be noticed.**

fairness principle. If an employee isn't willing to do the job, or cannot, you have to take steps. Sometimes discipline or termination is needed. Part of the job of keeping good employees involves weeding out bad ones.

*Fourth, apply the GRAPE theory,* a management style first outlined by Bill Scott, a professor at the University of New Hampshire's Thompson School of Applied Science who has spent more than 20 years studying small business management. His theory is about as untheoretical as you could wish. All employees have needs for:

- ☐ Growth
- ☐ Recognition
- ☐ Achievement
- ☐ Participation

To meet these needs, you (the owner) have to provide plenty of
- ☐ Effort.

The underpinning of the theory is that employees motivate themselves. Your job is to provide opportunities for them to exercise their skills and efforts.

1. *Growth* comes from training, from stretching skills and talents, from taking on more responsibility. Some growth opportunities come outside the business —amateur dramatics, learning to play a new sport or instrument, becoming a parent.

2. *Recognition.* One reason to provide periodic performance reviews is to make sure that you recognize your employees' contributions. Nobody likes to toil without being recognized—if their work is worth their hire, they want it to be noticed. If it needs improvement, fine. That's a form of recognition; it shows they aren't being overlooked. It's easy to forget the importance of this recognition factor. "Management by walking around" is effective because it provides chances to recognize employees' contributions and achievements. A small business is a perfect environment for this kind of management.

3. *Achievement.* A sense of achievement comes from doing something difficult —reaching a goal, helping the company gain a tough objective, mastering a new skill or machine, solving a problem. A well-managed business provides opportunities for achievement and growth, which can then be recognized (sincerely) and perhaps rewarded. Note the "sincerely": long-term, all recognition has to be based on achievement or else it degenerates into flattery, which will get you nowhere.

4. *Participation.* Remember the team analogy. One advantage a small business has over a big one is closeness to employees. You can involve them in their work life, and keep them constantly aware of how the business is doing. What are the company goals? Are we making progress? How can I contribute?

A lot of management practice centers on establishing a sense of participation: Look at management by objectives (in Chapter Nine), in which you and the employee set objectives together, establish dates to reach sub-goals en route to achieving the objectives, and agree on how to measure progress along the way. Sophisticated? Yes. Easy to do? Yes—if you take the time to provide the opportunity for your employees to participate in establishing and monitoring their own work. Who benefits? All of you.

5. *Effort*. It takes a lot of effort—consistent, attentive-to-detail effort from you and your employees. There is no substitute. As the owner, you have to provide the ongoing energy and direction that a business runs on. And that takes effort.

There are no magic management theories that effortlessly produce results. There are a number of proven tools you might wish to consider putting to work, though, in the GRAPE framework. Among these are:

| Tool | Description |
| --- | --- |
| Job enrichment | Add skills and responsibilities to a job. Make the job more challenging. Provides chance for growth, but may be hard to structure in a small company. |
| Job flexibility | Let employees structure their own jobs, go beyond the job description at their discretion. Works well with experienced workers but can leave some of the duller work undone. |
| Release time | Lets employees work on charitable or public efforts on company time, usually with pay. A great growth opportunity: for example, Community Chest is a training ground for managers, provides a strong sense of growth and achievement—to say nothing of the good will it creates for the company. Expensive, a ticklish situation for an employee with a bug in his bonnet, can create feelings of "why not me?" or "why not my charity or group?". |
| Special project | If well-designed, a terrific training tool. If not well-designed, expensive and interruptive. Make sure that the project contributes to company goals. |
| Objective setting | Involve employee in planning and goal-setting, especially for his or her own job. Make goals clear, attainable with effort, and measurable. (Increase sales $1,500/ month; increase profits $600/ month by January.) If done tactfully (some employees will set odd goals at first), a great tool with no downside. Be careful though: Employees often set unrealistically high goals, which is self-defeating and frustrating. |
| Suggestion programs | See Figure 6.1. The old suggestion box provides opportunities for achievement and recognition, especially when tied into a reward system and public applause. Make sure to get the suggestions in writing if possible, and make a swift reward following the "praise publicly, discipline privately" rule. Small rewards paid quickly work better than bigger |

| | but less frequent rewards. Everyone benefits. Make sure that the awards go to the right people. |
|---|---|
| Problem solving | Ask employees to help with problems, even if unrelated to their job. This implicit reliance on their input is invaluable. |
| Helping with change | Encourage employees to ask questions about big changes in the business (new equipment or facilities, products, ways of doing business). Actively encourage their participation in effecting the change and you defuse their fears and help them get used to the change. Incorporate their suggestions wherever possible. |

There are plenty of available tools to help your employees maintain their motivation. Any standard management textbook is full of them—but it comes down to treating your employees the way you would want to be treated yourself. Everyone wants honest appreciation and recognition of their efforts and contributions, respect as an individual, and opportunities for growth, recognition, achievement, and participation.

You and your employees are in this together—not enemies but partners. They may need leading, organizing and coordination (that's your job), but they will perform as well as they can if you don't get in their way.

This does call for planning and communicating on your part. Not easy or simple, but well within your reach.

---

Figure 8.1
**GRAPE Checklist**

Bill Scott provides this list of questions to help small business owners understand the elements of his GRAPE theory of management.

1.  **Growth**
    - ☐ Do you promote from within whenever possible?
    - ☐ Do you give good recommendations and help employees who leave for better jobs?
    - ☐ Do you train and encourage employees to learn about everything they can?
    - ☐ Do you institute and encourage workshops?
    - ☐ Do you pay partial tuition for schooling related to your company?
    - ☐ Do you counsel and initiate conversations to show employees how to improve or grow or develop a career?
    - ☐ Do you encourage membership in professional clubs or organizations?
    - ☐ Do you publicize promotions?
    - ☐ Do you explain to employees why someone has been brought in from outside? Show them how they can become as well qualified?
    - ☐ Do you rotate jobs among employees?
    - ☐ Do you use flexible work hours?

Figure 8.1 (cont.)

&#9633; Do you have a suggestion program?

&#9633; Do you use meaningful performance evaluations? See Chapter Nine.

## 2. Recognition

&#9633; Do you know when an employee does an exceptionally good job—and let him or her know you know?

&#9633; Do you know your employees' hobbies, interests, needs, and goals?

&#9633; Do you provide time to listen to individual employees?

&#9633; Do you meet with each employee for performance evaluations?

&#9633; Do you ask employees to help improve business operations?

&#9633; Do you help employees improve their skills?

## 3. Achievement

&#9633; Do you allow your employees chances to excel? To do the job their way?

&#9633; Do you explain what you want accomplished and allow your employees to figure out how to achieve those goals?

&#9633; Do you set assignments that stretch employees' abilities?

&#9633; Do you think your employees are capable of doing more or better work?

&#9633; Do you provide the tools, time, and other resources to improve their performance?

&#9633; Do you applaud their off-work achievements?

&#9633; Do you allow employees to use their heads in achieving your goals?

## 4. Participation

&#9633; Do you ask your employees' advice? Solicit their opinions?

&#9633; Do you implement their suggestions?

&#9633; Do you encourage employees to speak up?

&#9633; Do you practice listening?

&#9633; Can employees shape their work environment to some degree: hours, work groups, plants or pictures and so on?

&#9633; Do you use Management by Objectives? (MBO: See Chapter Nine.)

Periodically, review these questions. If most of them can be answered, "Yes," you are providing a working environment that allows employees to contribute more than 100% effort.

# Chapter Nine:
# What About Evaluations
# and Salary Reviews?

Performance evaluations are important for three reasons. First, they evaluate your employees' progress towards fulfilling the requirements of their jobs. Second, they'll ultimately help you improve your own business management skills. Third, they provide your employees with benchmarks, and give them a way to measure their own growth and achievements.

There are six basic steps in performance evaluations:

1.  *Prepare performance objectives with your employee,* based on (a) the job description, (b) your knowledge of the employee, (c) your understanding of the special circumstances (if any) your business is operating under. These include competition, condition of plant and equipment, general economic circumstances, and other factors. Do this alone, before meeting with your employee, so you have a framework.

2.  *Discuss the objectives with the employee.* Adjust them so both of you feel they are attainable, worth achieving, and measurable in the time frame involved. Explain how they help the company reach its goals.

3.  *Watch the employee's performance* during the time until the next evaluation (six months at the outside). If corrections are in order, suggest them.

    Provide training. If praise is in order, give it. Keep notes—with dates and details—to substantiate the evaluation.

4.  *Evaluate the performance against the objectives before the evaluation interview.* Fill out Figure 9.1: Employee Performance Evaluation, which can be found in Appendix One.

5.  *Discuss the evaluation with the employee. Be prepared to defend your evaluation with specifics;* the notes you have been taking (Step 3) will show the employee that you recognize his or her accomplishments, strengths, and shortcomings.

    For any rating with room for improvement—all have room because nobody is perfect—ask the employee how the performance could be improved. Since most employees know that they could do better in certain parts of their job, this won't be threatening. Your aim is to improve performance so your business can achieve its goals.

6.  *Now take whatever action is appropriate.* If the employee deserves praise, provide it. If the employee just doesn't fit in with your business, consider firing him or her. See Chapter Ten for the specific steps to follow. Most of the time, though, the appropriate action will consist of setting new objectives with the employee for the next evaluation period, suggesting training

**Performance evaluations are a great source of information for ways to improve the entire business, not just the employee's performance.**

or other opportunities for higher performance, and helping the employee get ready for more responsible or challenging work.

If you listen to your employee, some problems may be brought up that you were unaware of: Perhaps productivity is flat because a machine has too much downtime, or a parts bin has been moved to an inconvenient spot, or sales are down because of stockouts. Performance evaluations are a great source of information for ways to improve the entire business, not just the employee's performance.

Sometimes an employee will be defensive. That's one reason to be prepared with as many factual, dated observations as possible. There is no substitute for a comment such as, "You had an argument with a customer June 3, and another one August 5. Do you think you can change that response, even when the customer is wrong?"

Performance evaluations work for a lot of reasons. They help set goals, provide a means to improve performance (growth) and reach objectives (achievement), are a clear form of recognition, and—if approached as a joint effort—give a strong sense of participation.

Note that the performance review does not include salary. The last step—taking appropriate action—may include granting a raise (or withholding one). But it may not. Ideally, the salary review is a separate issue, based on performance but also including other factors such as the employee's seniority, contribution to other company goals, and even the employee's needs. While a small business cannot build in automatic pay raises, almost all do. Employees expect raises—and employers seem to expect to give them.

### Salary Reviews

When you establish salary ranges (see Chapter Six), with a ±10% range, you tacitly set a limit on what a job is worth to your business. Keep these averages and ranges current. They change, sometimes dramatically, and you don't want to be caught in a rigid posture with outdated numbers.

Some factors that you may want to consider in deciding on salary increases are:

☐ Company profits and budgets. Salaries are fixed costs.

☐ Seniority has a place—long-term loyal employees contribute in more than the obvious ways.

☐ Two small salary increases per year have a more positive effect than one bigger increase, and are less painful to your cash flow. A raise of $10 a week in January and another $10 in June adds up to $780 for the year. A raise of $20 a week in March also adds $780 to the outflow, but the employee will usually feel that it's a long time between pay raises. (And a $20 raise in January amounts to $1,040 per year.)

☐ If you keep your employees aware of the financial condition of your business, they may be less demanding when times are tight. Most people prefer a secure job—and if the wages are fair, will postpone a raise to help the business.

☐ There are non-cash raises you might offer instead of (or with) more normal raises: time off, extra holidays, help with tuition, a change in job structure, more flexible hours.

☐ People are as sensitive about salaries as about any topic that affects their lives. Make sure that salary information is private—but also make sure that salaries reflect contribution to the business. An unfair salary range, where two people get very different pay for no apparent reason, is a major source of employee anger; it can also present legal problems. Keep the fairness principle in mind.

☐ During a salary review, point out the value of the fringe benefits, and keep the employee aware of increases in these benefits. A salary review is a compensation review. Use Figure 6.3 to drive the value of the fringe benefits home.

## Promotions

The performance review is a good time to discuss promotion possibilities. While small businesses do not have a lot of promotion possibilities—a three-employee business, for example, with an owner and two employees has little room for a "promotion"—every business can provide new challenges. A job can be given added dimensions: more responsibility, higher goals, more employee control over working conditions, outside research or sales effort. A good promotion substitute is release time: "If you can get your job done by 3:00 on Wednesday, you can work on your club fund raiser."

If you can provide a real promotion, and the employee is qualified and willing to accept the promotion, great. There are few morale boosters as strong as the chance to be promoted on the basis of actual performance and contribution to the business. Once more: Promotions based on other grounds will be seen as unfair, and cause endless problems. Be fair.

Treat a promotion the same way you treat a new hire: Make sure the best person gets the job. A qualified employee has a huge advantage over an outsider: familiarity with the business. You know how the employee works and deals with responsibility, and you can train the employee to fit the new job description.

☐ Make sure you have an up-to-date job description for both the new position the employee will have and for the position the employee is leaving.

☐ Be prepared to fill the vacated job—from within (another promotion possibility) if possible. Promoting an employee alters work patterns, leaving some duties uncovered. Be careful.

**A qualified employee has a huge advantage over an outsider: familiarity with the business.**

69

**Your objective is to identify strengths and weaknesses, correct or applaud as soon as possible, maintain a fair, factual basis for promotions and salary increases, and to help your business attain the objectives you set for it.**

☐ Treat the newly promoted person as a new hire: go through the parts of the orientation procedure that make the most sense (use your judgment). Changing work and peer relationships can be very difficult, and the newly promoted person will need support.

☐ If other people thought they should have received (or been considered for) the promotion, make sure they understand that you chose the person best matched to the requirements of the job. If you always promote fairly, no problem. If the promotion is based on other grounds, you may find yourself open to legal action.

☐ Follow up on the newly promoted person—at the end of the first week, after a few weeks on the job, and after a month. Be available in between times; this is particularly important if the person now is managing other people. Look for training needs—and provide the required training.

☐ Salary increases and promotions go together. Fortunately, you can tie the increase to performance, setting objectives and timing to achieve those objectives with the newly promoted employee. Remember: A small raise now, and another small one in six months is more appreciated than a larger raise infrequently administered.

☐ As you and the newly promoted person set objectives together, be prepared for some unrealistic expectations. Don't be surprised, for example, to have the employee set goals that cannot be reached (enthusiasm is great), but temper the goals with your experience and understanding of the business as gently as possible. Again, provide facts. If the employee wants to spend $100,000 to gain a $10,000 sales increase, let him or her down gently.

Performance evaluations and promotions are among the best morale boosting and motivation sustaining tools you have. They also are a strong defense against incompetence: If you have five employees, and one of them is underproducing, 20% of your work force is a problem. If that one person reduces the productivity of others by 25% (by complaining, being late, interrupting work flow or waiting on too few customers), you have about a 40% loss.

So keep the evaluations constant, objective, factual and fair. Your objective is not to find fault and hoard up notes to blast employees with—it's to identify strengths and weaknesses, correct or applaud as soon as possible, maintain a fair, factual basis for promotions and salary increases, and to help your business attain the objectives you set for it.

The principle is simple: Periodically, meet privately with each employee to review their progress, recognize their growth and achievements, and let them participate in setting objectives which will be used to evaluate their performance. Measurable and dated facts are needed, both to correct or alter behaviors and to leverage strengths. If, for example, you find that the stockboy has a gift for sales, make a note. Praise him at the time—publicly, if you wish—and drop a note in his file. At review time, suggest a sales course, some OJT, or a new position. You can get a new stockboy more easily than a new salesperson, provide another example of promotion from within, and benefit everyone.

Do not use the performance evaluation to blow off an accumulation of grievances. The employee will be defensive anyway (certainly apprehensive). The best time to correct a behavior is as soon as the problem arises, in private. Keep notes. If the behavior remains improved, cite it as a positive change: "You had arguments with customers in June and August; I see you've had none since. Good work."

By setting objectives and performance evaluation criteria with the employee, you accomplish a number of important management goals. GRAPE, and its accompanying management by objective style, works. It provides the benchmarks needed to chart improvement, helps employees stretch their abilities, provides another channel of communication, and helps maintain the sense of fairness and equity that everyone wants.

It also keeps the standards open. Arbitrary standards dictated by management are less helpful than arriving at those same standards by discussing them with the employees involved.

**Management by Objectives**

Management by objectives (MBO) is an augmented performance evaluation tool in which the employee participates in setting goals and objectives, and has input into the means to attain those goals. Figure 9.2: Preliminary Goal Setting will help implement this powerful management tool.

MBO requires that you:
- [ ] Know what you want the employee to accomplish;
- [ ] Inform the employee of your expectations;
- [ ] Observe and evaluate the employee's performance;
- [ ] Discuss that evaluation with the employee; and
- [ ] Take action.

MBO proceeds in six straightforward steps.

*Step One: Update the job description with the employee's help.* By doing this together—which is time-consuming—you gain the employee's cooperation. You might want to start with a very sketchy job description, then fill it in with the employee's help. The review and insights provided by your employee are valuable in themselves; your employees are closer to their jobs than you are. For a new employee, however, be more directive—he/she doesn't know the job as well as you do.

*Step Two: Draft a statement of the objectives.* Figure 9.2 helps—get the employee to fill one out too. When you sit down together to set the objectives for the quarter or for a six-month period, you will both be prepared.

This doesn't mean that you let the employee take over your management prerogatives. Far from it—you have to revise and focus the objectives to fit in with other company goals. But you are saying, loud and clear, that you expect the employee to think, be creative, become involved, and take charge of his or her job.

**Your aim is to build a mutually acceptable set of measurable, time-bound objectives that, if attained, further the company's overall growth.**

**Studies show that employees set goals that are unrealistically high most of the time.**

Your aim is to build a mutually acceptable set of measurable, time-bound objectives that, if attained, further the company's overall goals.

*Step Three: Review the employee's draft with the employee.* "Open covenants openly arrived at" was a good political ideal. It's an employer/employee relationship ideal, too.

Encourage the employee by taking his or her ideas seriously. There are three possibilities here:

- ☐ The employee sets goals that are too high;
- ☐ The employee sets goals that are too low; or
- ☐ The employee sets goals that agree with yours.

Studies show that employees set goals that are unrealistically high most of the time. Such goals are frustrating. Negotiate them downward.

In the second case, be firm. You usually know which employees will set low goals. To raise them, focus on the goals, not the person. "I see a 5% increase as the goal here...maybe that's not giving you enough credit; how about 12%?" is better than "You always set low goals..."

Sometimes you'll have to dictate the goals—but rarely. More often, discussion of how the goal was set, why you think it could be higher, and perhaps comparison with other goals or statistics will gain agreement. Sometimes employees are down on themselves, and need encouragement: "I bet you could gain that 12%...How can I help you?"

If the objectives coincide, rejoice. Find out how the employee reached those objectives, see about making a marginal improvement in them, and compare your goal-setting methods with the employee's.

These three steps set up the MBO practice. During the next quarter or six months, observe and monitor progress towards the objectives.

*Step Four: Have the employee draft his or her own performance appraisal.* Since you and the employee both know what was expected, this is a book-keeping task. What is of most interest to you is the comment section: Why did the employee meet or fail to meet the objectives? Figure 9.3 provides a framework for this.

Figure 9.2
# Preliminary Goal Setting

**I. Performance Objectives: Employee Preliminary Goals**

Employee: _AB_      Date proposed: _6/21/86_

For period: _6/86_ to _1/87_      To be reviewed: _by AB on 1/1/87_

Basic job description (Attach copy if available):

_See attached_

**II. Objectives I Can Realistically Accomplish**

(Example:100% accuracy is not realistic; improvement from 90% accuracy to 95% may be.)

1. _Increase sales 8% by 9/86 ; by 12% by 1/87_
2. _Hold costs to current levels_
3. _Finish Tucson project_
4. _Finish CAC project_
5. _Get Board of Directors assembled_
6. _Refinance division (?)_
7.
8.

**III. Measurement of Success**

(Example: Dollar amount, hours, percentages of measurable quantities, averages.)

1. _Sales from $45 to $48 by 9/1/86_
2. _Sales from $48 to $54 by 1/1/87_
3. _Deliver roughs by 1/1/87 to Tucson_
4. _CAC by 7/86_
5. _Board by 9/86_
6. _Finance in progress_
7.
8.

**IV. In Order to Accomplish These Objectives I Need the Following:**

(Examples: additional tools, time, money, training, personnel and so forth.)

1. _Budget for sales and marketing_
2. _New sales plan_
3. _Direct sales rep a possibility_
4.
5.
6.
7.
8.

**MBO helps employees make contributions to the company beyond the average, boosts morale, and sets up a feedback system for checking progress.**

Figure 9.3
**Performance Appraisal**

Employee name: *AB*    Date: *9/6/86*

Objective:        Results:        Comments:

*Increase*       *Increased*      *Lost one major*
*Sales by*       *Sales 3%*       *account; will*
*8%*                              *replace within 30*
                                 *days (signed contracts with*
                                 *three new banks)*

The objectives come straight from Figure 9.2; results are based on performance, and the comments provide the kind of information you want to improve performance in the future. Save these forms; they are a source of ideas for future business improvements.

*Step Five: Discuss the results with the employee.* Keep your ears open and your mouth shut; you want to learn, and that means you have to listen to the employee. Ask questions, but don't provide the answers. Try to find out how and why objectives were or were not attained. Maybe the reasons are external to the business: competition, economics, legal changes. Maybe they are beyond the employee's control: changes in company strategies, machine failure, change in vendors, lack of advertising and marketing efforts. The aim is not to be punitive, but to make those objectives attainable in the future.

Note the importance of communication throughout this process. When you review the employee's performance appraisal with the employee, try to elicit training, equipment, or other needs. Sometimes employees are shy about asking for help.

Listen. And ask. And listen some more. Provide praise and encouragement; make sure the employee knows you recognize his or her efforts.

*Step Six: Start over again.* Get out the job description; update it.

MBO may not be the best method for everyone, but in small companies it is particularly powerful. It helps employees make contributions to the company beyond the average, boosts morale, and sets up a feedback system for checking progress.

No management tool can do more than that.

# Chapter Ten:
# What Do I Do with Problem Employees?

How you deal with a problem employee depends—on the employee, on the cause of the problem, on the problem itself. It depends on the amount of factual information (dated, objective information—written down and saved) you have about the employee's behavior. It depends on what procedures you have established (either deliberately or through habitual practice) to deal with problem employees.

The legal ramifications can be severe. So can the economic consequences. FUTA and state unemployment taxes may skyrocket. You may need legal help at $125/hour, or find that a former employee is badmouthing your business and causing problems that will have a price tag later.

Dealing with problem employees really means dealing with problem behaviors. Unless you are a professionally trained counselor, your job is not concerned with the problem employee but with the problems the employee's behavior is causing your business.

*Step One: Before taking any action, try to determine what kind of problem you are dealing with.* Employee problems fall into two broad categories: inefficiencies and misconduct.

Inefficiencies can be corrected by training, job reorganization, rescheduling, or transferring the employee to a job better matched to his or her capabilities.

Misconduct problems are less tractable. Procedures for handling inefficiencies are clear. The preceding chapters set up review procedures and suggested methods of handling problems due to inefficiencies. Employee misconduct problems are harder to handle. Some are due to outside pressures—maybe a marital or family problem, or a difficult neighbor, or a poor investment that causes a lot of concern. It may be due to a job related problem: a personality conflict, trouble with a customer, pressure from other workers, boredom with the current job, inability to handle the pressure.

Or it may be substance abuse or other psychological or emotional problems.

If you approach an employee who is exhibiting bizarre or destructive behavior—habitual tardiness or absenteeism, rudeness to customers, inability to concentrate—and concentrate on the behavior rather than the person, most of the time the employee will respond positively.

If the behavior poses a danger to anyone, put safety first and don't hesitate to call in professional help. Otherwise, follow a written, well-communicated disciplinary procedure. See Figures 10.1 and 10.2 for some guidelines.

**Your job is not concerned with the problem employee but with the problems the employee's behavior is causing your business.**

# Figure 10.1
## Disciplinary Guidelines

| Incident | Offense | | | |
|---|---|---|---|---|
| | First | Second | Third | Fourth |
| 1. Absent, no call | O | O | W | F |
| 2. Walking off job, no reason or notice given | O | W | F | |
| 3. Arguing with employee(s) | O | W | SW | F |
| 4. Arguing with customer | O | W | SW | F |
| 5. Fighting with employee or fighting with customer | O | SW | F | |
| 6. Intimidation, harassment (sexual or other) of employee | O | SW | F | |
| 7. Insubordination | O | O | W | SW |
| 8. Purposeful destruction of company property | W | F | | |
| 9. Theft | W | F | | |
| 10. Possession or sale of illegal drugs or alcohol on company property | W | SW | F | |
| 11. Intoxication or under the influence of illegal drugs on company property | W | SP | SW | F |
| 12. Ignoring safety rules | W | SP | SW | F |

Key:  O = oral reminder     W = written reminder          SP = suspend with pay
SW = suspend without pay     F = fire

Fill in the appropriate blanks for your business.

If the problem is inefficency, due to outside pressure or to the job, try to find the cause of the problem. Sometimes it will solve itself; sometimes just sharing a problem with another person provides needed relief.

But if you suspect the problem to be substance abuse, proceed with a lot of caution. Substance abusers will often deny that their problem is alcohol or some other drug related problem, and are extraordinarily good at laying the blame on other people. Get professional help. Employee Assistance Plans (EAPs) are becoming more common and more affordable. If none is available in your area, call the local Alcoholics Anonymous number and ask what they recommend—they will know what assistance is available.

Figure 10.1, Disciplinary Guidelines, is not totally rigid. It's a guideline that you can post or give to all employees. People like to know what the limits are, and if you have to proceed to the more drastic steps (suspension, firing), an outline such as this helps everyone understand the rules.

*Step Two (A): If the problem is inefficiency, it stems from a mismatch between the employee and the job, usually a lack of skills or training.* In these cases, review the job standards, point out the unsatisfactory performance, and see if additional time or training solves the problem.

If it doesn't, transfer the employee or change the job. You want to show good faith in case the employee has to be fired, which is a last resort.

Make sure that all employees are subject to the same rules. And be fair: You can't have one set of standards for one employee and a different set for another without courting legal trouble.

*Step Two (B): If the problem is misconduct—intentional and willful or "repeatedly negligent" behavior—communicate the work rules, advise and carefully define the violations in question, and attempt to change the behavior with progressively more intense discipline (see Figure 10.2 on page 79).*

If this doesn't work, provide whatever review procedure you have established before firing the person. Once again, you have to be fair, make a good faith attempt to salvage the situation—and then you can get rid of the problem employee. Your review procedure may be as simple as the employee meeting offsite with you—but it must be the same for all employees.

*Step Three: In either case, make sure to thoroughly and completely document your side of the story.* Unfortunately, it's true that as the employer you have to lean over backwards to protect your company (and even your personal assets) against legal actions that make little or no sense. Knowing that, protect yourself. The procedures you should follow are designed to show that you have made a good faith attempt to provide equal and consistent treatment for all of your employees.

For minor problems such as chronic tardiness or excessive absenteeism, the cure is to make sure that the employee knows his or her contribution to the company is important. Usually an oral reminder and attention to their response is all that you have to do; if the problem persists, then begin to bring in the steps outlined above.

Provide a clear disciplinary process and follow it. Make no exceptions that can't be justified. Chronic troublemakers don't stick around where procedures are clear and consistent—and they can't cause problems for you later if you maintain clear records of dates, names, and facts to support your side of the argument.

**Provide a clear disciplinary process and follow it. Make no exceptions that can't be justified.**

Figure 10.2
# Handling a Problem Employee

Follow this checklist when a problem arises that you think will lead to progressively more serious disciplinary actions. Keep notes—with dates— to substantiate the content of discussions and counseling efforts.
**Name of employee:**

**Describe behavior(s):**

                                                                    **Date, Initials**

☐  Employee notified of performance and behavior standards          _____

☐  Oral reminders                                                   _____

For minor incidents, use oral reminders immediately. Don't store grievances. Solve the problem instead. Collect and evaluate facts—not feelings or assumptions—and make notes covering dates and results.

If the problem persists for a single moderate incident or if the employee fails to respond to several oral reminders:

☐  State the violation clearly, in writing, with dates, names, facts (no hearsay, anger, or phrases which could be interpreted as insults). Review with the offending employee, get his/her signature, give him/her a copy, and keep the original for your files.

The next step is either a suspension or a final written notice. Reserve this for either a single incident of severe misconduct or for a final warning to improve.

☐  Advise the person that his or her job and income are in immediate danger.
☐  Suspend with pay if the facts are in doubt; investigate thoroughly.
☐  Give the employee a copy of the final written notice. Keep the original for your files.

If it is necessary to fire the employee:

☐  Make sure to have a valid business reason, based on facts and documented to make sure the procedure has been fair.
☐  If there is any doubt, ask your lawyer's advice.
☐  Prepare the paperwork: last paycheck, other personnel documents (such as insurance notification). Be sure your records illustrate the steps taken as outlined above.
☐  Prepare for the exit interview. See Figure 10.3. It is often advisable to have another person present. Select the time and place for privacy.
☐  Notify the employee. Ordinarily he or she is expecting to be fired, but be prepared for either anger or tears. Keep it businesslike, make it final, and notify them of any appeal procedure they might follow. In a small business where you are the appeal procedure, this is still important. Let the employee respond.
☐  Finish off all loose ends: Arrange return of company keys, and other property; explain severance pay and insurance procedures.

Your objective remains the same: to treat this employee fairly and to show that you made every reasonable effort to remedy the problem. Do this, and you're <u>probably</u> legally covered. ("<u>Probably</u>" is underlined as a warning: As mentioned earlier, courts take somewhat erratic views. When in any doubt at all, check with your lawyer.)

Figure 10.3
# Exit Interview

Employee _____ Title _____

Last day worked _____

Please check the following appropriately:

| | Excellent | Good | Fair | Poor | Comments |
|---|---|---|---|---|---|
| 1. How were our working conditions? | ☐ | ☐ | ☐ | ☐ | |
| 2. How was your compensation? | ☐ | ☐ | ☐ | ☐ | |
| 3. How well are tasks and employees matched? | ☐ | ☐ | ☐ | ☐ | |
| 4. How well was work organized? | ☐ | ☐ | ☐ | ☐ | |
| 5. What did you feel your growth potential was? | ☐ | ☐ | ☐ | ☐ | |
| 6. What did you feel your opportunity was to participate, make suggestions, be involved in your work? | ☐ | ☐ | ☐ | ☐ | |
| 7. How well did you receive recognition or credit for your contributions? | ☐ | ☐ | ☐ | ☐ | |
| 8. How did management treat you? | ☐ | ☐ | ☐ | ☐ | |

9. My major reason for leaving is: _____

_____

10. Can you make any suggestions as to how the company could be a better place in which to work?

_____

_____

11. Remarks: _____

_____

_____

Forwarding Address:



Date_____ Company representative interviewing employee _____

Fill out this form with the departing employees. If the employee is leaving for a better position or a different challenge, or is retiring voluntarily, this is a good oportunity for you to elicit objective, constructive criticism.

If the separation is not amicable, you should still conduct an exit interview. You give the employee an opportunity to vent his/her anger, and a structure in which to provide specific criticisms. This way, you (the employer) gain insight into sources of employee disatisfaction. You also diffuse a potentially hostile situation.

# Chapter Eleven:
# What About Pension Plans?

Pension and retirement plans are major fringe benefits which help you attract and retain good personnel.

As the owner of your company, you probably think of your business as your retirement plan. To some extent it is—but to protect yourself and your family, set aside separate funds for your retirement and do not rely solely on your business.

Ownership of a small business is the best tax shelter of all—one which won't be taken away by any proposed tax legislation. This provides a variety of ways to save for retirement:

☐ Increase the value of the business preparatory to selling it on retirement. This is the best method—but not the safest.

☐ Hedge your bets, and complement your retirement funds with insurance. Ask your insurance agent and accountant about split-dollar plans.

☐ Set up a pension plan, either contributory where the employees (including you) make predefined contributions to the plan's cost, or non-contributory where the company bears the total cost of the plan.

For employees, the question of pensions and retirement plans is more pressing: Most small businesses do not offer pensions or retirement plans, leaving the employees to fend for themselves. While IRAs can help, many employees will not be able to take advantage of them, and will have to eventually fall back on Social Security.

What can you do to help them? Retirement plans are highly complex and are regulated by a very stringent set of laws. These plans must be set up by professionals.

What's in it for you—the owner? As your work force gets older, their interest in retirement increases. They can read papers and watch TV, and see how small the Social Security benefits are. If you can afford a pension or retirement plan which includes all qualified employees, and there are ways you can, you will retain and reward your most valued employees.

### Types of Retirement Plans

There are three kinds of qualified retirement plans available to owners of incorporated and unincorporated businesses and their employees: defined benefit plans, defined contribution plans, and Simplified Employee Pension (SEP) plans. These plans must:

*(text continued on page 84)*

**To protect yourself and your family, set aside separate funds for your retirement and do not rely solely on your business.**

Figure 11.1

## Comparing Retirement Plans

| Type of Plan | **Who**<br>Can Participate in One | **How Much**<br>Can Be Contributed | **When**<br>Funds May Be Taken Out |
|---|---|---|---|
| **Individual Retirement Account (IRA)** | All people who earn current wages; all married couples as long as one spouse earns wages. | $2,000 or 100% of earned income, whichever is less, for all wage-earners; $2,250 for spousal accounts. | Can begin as early as age 59 1/2 and must begin no later than age 70 1/2. |
| **Simplified Employee Pension (SEP) Plan** | All self-employed individuals, owners of unincorporated and incorporated businesses, and their employees. | Employers contribute up to the lesser of $7,000 or 15% of compensation to employees' SEP-IRAs. | Same as above. |
| **Defined Benefit Plan** | Same as above. | Contributions that will produce the lesser of $90,000 or 100% of salary for annual pension benefit, if you retire at age 65. If you retire earlier, your benefit is reduced. | If employment ceases prior to retirement, funds may be rolled over without being taxed to another pension/profit-sharing plan or to an IRA, with certain limitations. |
| **Defined Contribution Plan** | Same as above. | The lesser of $30,000 or 25% of compensation. | Same as above; and in-service withdrawal permitted within narrow circumstances. |
| **401 (k) or Deferred Compensation Savings Plan** | All owners of incorporated businesses and their employees. | Up to $7,000, less the amount contributed to any other qualified retirement plan. | Same as above; and in-service withdrawal permitted within narrow circumstances. |

Figure 11.1 *(continued)*

| Type of Plan | Advantages | Restrictions |
|---|---|---|
| **Individual Retirement Account (IRA)** | •Current federal income tax deduction if income does not exceed certain levels or if taxpayer does not participate in an employer-sponsored plan. •Funds grow deferred from both federal and state current taxes. | •Substantial penalties for early withdrawals and for failure to make minimum withdrawals after age 70 1/2. •No "five-year-forward averaging" to reduce the tax bite on lump-sum withdrawals. |
| **Simplified Employee Pension (SEP) Plan** | •Employer's contribution is tax-deductible to both employer and employees. •Employees can make an additional deductible contribution of the lesser of 100% compensation or $2,000 to an IRA with certain limitations. •No minimum annual contribution requirement. | Same as above. |
| **Defined Benefit Plan** | •Participants retire with a fixed, determinable benefit. •Investment income grows free from taxes. •"Five-year-forward averaging" can reduce tax bite on lump-sum withdrawals. •Employees may have IRAs and participate in other pension/profit-sharing plans, with certain limitations. | •Higher administrative fees. •More complicated to administer. |
| **Defined Contribution Plan** | •Employers and, if the plan allows, employees contribute a fixed percentage each year. •"Five-year-forward averaging" can reduce tax bite on lump-sum withdrawals. •Employees may have IRAs and participate in other pension/profit-sharing plans, within certain limits. | Benefits received at retirement depend on investment performance. |
| **401 (k) or Deferred Compensation Savings Plan** | •Employees pay no federal income tax on the portion of their salary contributed to a 401(k). •Employers may match employees' contribution within certain limits. •Income earned accumulates tax-free until withdrawal. •Participants may have IRAs and, within certain limits, participate in other pension/profit-sharing plans. •"Five-year-forward averaging" can reduce tax bite on lump-sum withdrawals. | Same as above; and a 10% penalty, on top of any income tax owed, is imposed upon withdrawals taken before retirement. |

83

*(text continued from page 81)*

☐ Be a legally binding written contract;

☐ Be for the exclusive benefit of the employees and their beneficiaries; and

☐ Benefit a broad class of employees and not discriminate in favor of officers, stockholders, or highly-paid employees.

Qualified plans define, in advance, the rights and benefits of participants as well as eligibility qualifications. They must also include an employee's trust to contain contributions and preserve the tax advantages.

The advantages of formal plans are: Costs can be calculated in advance; there are many tax advantages; costs are distributed over a lengthy period; and in most cases trust fund contributions are safeguarded from creditors.

Most banks have Master Trust plans to handle the detailed paperwork and necessary legal work, and make the appropriate changes to ensure continued compliance with the laws. The main drawback for most small business owners are the costs involved.

What are your choices? Defined Benefit Plans, Defined Contribution Plans, and SEPs. (Figure 11.1 compares these plans with IRAs and 401(k) plans, which may only be set up by incorporated businesses.) Each has advantages and disadvantages—check with your accountant and the trust department of your bank for the most recent details. The following pages will help you outline the choices for you and your business. But: Make sure to check with your accountant and lawyer.

*1. Defined Benefit Plans have certain advantages for stable businesses.*

Contributions to defined benefit plans are contingent on the assumed employee retirement benefit, usually calculated as a percentage of pre-retirement income. Contributions will vary from one employee to another, depending on years to retirement, income levels, and eligibility requirements. An actuary will determine the amounts due each year.

Once you adopt a given formula, benefits can be provided in proportion to length of service, amount of salary, or any non-discriminatory method. The following are some frequently chosen benefit formulas:

☐ Fixed percentage formula directly reflects pre-retirement income: e.g., 50% of last three year's average salary.

☐ Flat amount formula provides a given benefit to all participants, e.g. $250 per month.

☐ Unit benefit formula provides a pension equal to a percentage of salary for each year of service.

☐ Social Security integrated formula allows you to offset your contribution with Social Security benefits.

*2. Defined Contribution Plans can be helpful since you can forego contributions in low profit years without jeopardizing the plan.* These also favor companies with younger stockholders or employees, who stand to accrue greater benefits from more years of service.

Qualified profit-sharing plans are based on contributions from business profits to an employee trust based on one or a combination of three formulas:

- ☐ flat percentage of profits;
- ☐ percentage of profits above a minimum level;
- ☐ increased contributions with increased profits.

The formula may not discriminate in favor of stockholders or highly-paid employees—but may relate to employee income and length of service.

Money Purchase Pension Plans require you to annually set aside a defined amount in a pension fund. An employee may add to that amount if the plan is contributory. Typically, the plan's formula will express the employer's contribution as a percentage of the annual payroll of the participants. Funds are allocated to the employees on a pro rata basis.

A defined contribution plan is **not** the best idea for older corporate owners, but is excellent for younger participants.

Target Benefit Plans (also called assumed or variable benefit pension plans) are a combination of money purchase and defined benefit plans. Benefits are determined by a benefit formula, but the ultimate retirement benefit fluctuates with pension fund earnings and/or changes in the cost of living index.

*3. Simplified Employee Pension (SEP) Plans allow you to make contributions to your employee's Individual Retirement Account (IRA).* You can tie your contribution to company profits, but once again you must not discriminate against or in favor of any one group.

To establish a SEP, you must execute a written instrument that includes the name of the company, requirements for employee participation, and a formula that outlines the requirements an employee must satisfy in order to share in the allocation. This calls for professional help.

For every calendar year that the company contributes to the plan, a contribution must be made for each employee, age 21 or older, who has worked for your company any part of at least three of the past five calendar years and has earned at least $300 in the current year. Employees are immediately vested in their contributions, which cannot be conditioned on their remaining in the SEP account.

**A defined contribution plan is not the best idea for older corporate owners, but is excellent for younger participants.**

**ERISA does not require an employer to set up a retirement plan—but does require existing plans to meet certain minimum standards.**

---

Figure 11.2

## ERISA

If you decide to establish a retirement or pension plan, make sure that your advisors are thoroughly familiar with ERISA (Employee Retirement Income Security Act) and the other major tax laws affecting pension plans.

ERISA, enacted on Labor Day 1974, is administered by the Department of Labor, the IRS, and the Pension Benefit Guaranty Corporation. Its main tenet is that everyone may put aside funds, on a tax-deferred basis, for retirement.

ERISA safeguards over 40,000,000 workers (no government employees) and their beneficiaries, whether the employee participates in a private retirement plan, is self-employed, or has no job-relateed coverage other than Social Security.

ERISA does not require an employer to set up a retirement plan—but does require existing plans to meet certain minimum standards.

Since ERISA was passed, five major tax laws have further refined its provisions:
1. Economic Recovery Tax Act of 1981 (ERTA);
2. Tax Equity and Fiscal Responsibility Act of 1982 (TEFRA);
3. Deficit Reduction Act of 1983;
4. Retirement Equity Act of 1983; and
5. Tax Reform Act of 1986.

---

This is the most helpful plan for small corporations—but check carefully with your professional advisors.

Your best tax shelter remains your business. Build the business—but hedge your bets and fund your own and your employees' retirement. The costs are far lower than the benefits.

You must have professional advisors to be sure that you do not run afoul of these regulations—and to make sure that you set up the right plan for your business, your employees, and yourself.

# Chapter Twelve:
# What Happens When I Retire?

Too many small businesses die when their owners die or retire because no provision has been made for succession—for a person to take over the business and continue to run it profitably.

Sometimes the reason for failure is financial: inadequate key man insurance, for example. More often the reason is unwillingness to relinquish authority.

The financial aspects of succession planning are straightforward:

☐ Review insurance coverage: key man, cross-purchase, and perhaps disability. Succession plans may be needed sooner than you expect.

☐ Ask your accountant to place and maintain an IRS-defensible value on the business for tax and estate purposes. This can tie in with the insurance coverages; if you were to die or become disabled, what happens?

☐ If you have a valid valuation of the business, many of the problems (emotional as well as business) involved in selling the business you have fought to establish will be diminished. An unreal expectation (for example, the emotionally fraught "My business is worth $1 million") can make succession impossible.

☐ The assets of the business will be used by the buyer to finance the purchase. Make sure to have records, tax returns, and other information up to date at all times, to support the valuation placed on the assets. This is especially important for the less tangible items: market position, customer lists, "good will."

☐ Ask your accountant to suggest ways to build up cash or cash equivalents in the business to help fund an employee buyout of your equity.

☐ Keep your banker well informed of your plans. If you are going to retire in six months, let your banker know—to ensure continued bank support of the business once you are gone.

☐ One of the best succession plans you can have is your business plan. It provides the direction and tactical steps to keep the business going until such time as a new owner can take over completely. Keep a written business plan. An annual update should be sufficient.

The more difficult aspect of succession planning is coming to grips with the fact that you won't always be running your business. At some point, you have to turn the reins over to another person.

**The more difficult aspect of succession planning is coming to grips with the fact that you won't always be running your business.**

There are many reasons for wanting to make sure that you have a successor:

□ *Personal reasons.* Maybe you'd like to take an extended vacation, a long trip, or time off for other personal reasons. If you have an employee who can fill in for you, you aren't tied to the business year after year.

□ *Security.* If you become disabled, who will run the business and keep your salary coming in? Or provide income to your beneficiaries if you die?

□ *Continuity.* You've spent a lot of time and worry building up your business—and probably want it to continue. Maybe you have a son, daughter, or a trusted employee you want to pass the business to.

□ *Concern for your employees.* You can't have a successful business with lackluster employees—and you probably feel a sense of obligation toward them. Once you aren't running the business, what happens to them?

□ *Maximizing the value of the business.* If you plan to sell the business so you can retire in comfort, building a strong team to continue the business is an excellent investment. If you sell to your employees—as many business owners do—you will be taking back paper for a large part of the selling price. Tax and cash flow considerations dictate this; do you want your paper protected by a capable manager, or would you rather leave it to chance?

How do you begin planning for a successor?

*Step One: Determine your goals.* If you plan to work for another five years, that helps set a time frame. If you plan to work until you drop, better start planning soon—you never know, and unless you have a backup, you are taking unnecessary risks.

*Step Two: What do you do that nobody else in the business can do? Update your own job description.* List all of the things you do—however trivial they may appear—for a few weeks. Then go over them and for each one ask:
□ Is this important?
□ Can I delegate this task? (If yes, delegate it.)
□ How can someone else get experience in this?
□ Does it have to be done at all—or can it be done another way?

*Step Three: What about key employees—those who would be hardest to replace?* You have to include them in succession planning. If they have to be replaced, it will be at the least convenient time. Have each of them go over their own job description, asking the same kinds of questions you asked of your own job in Step Two.

*Step Four: Once you have a handle on what skills you bring to your business, and what skills are needed to continue the business (which may be different; see Figure 12.1 for some ideas), outline how you would find a replacement for yourself:*

☐  Look inside your business. Is there anyone who, with experience and grooming, could take over?
☐  Write up a job description for your successor.
☐  If you plan to be succeeded by one of your children, what skills must they develop? How can this best be done?
☐  If your successor is a non-related employee, how can his or her skills be developed? What training would be needed?

*Step Five: Write down a succession plan, covering the following areas:*

☐  A timetable for developing your successor's skills;
☐  Ideas on who your successor should be; and
☐  What resources are available to help your successor—banker, accountant, lawyer, other advisors. If you have a Board of Directors, this is something they should help with.

*Step Six: Delegate as much of your job as possible—the more experience your successor has, the better.* This can be ticklish: Letting someone else make decisions that affect your business is hard. But it has to be done; pseudo-delegation doesn't accomplish anything except to frustrate and anger the person whose decisions you second guess. Let people make mistakes—it's the best way for them to learn. (Then have them rectify their errors—that's the second best way.)

**Pseudo-delegation doesn't accomplish anything except to frustrate and anger the person whose decisions you second guess.**

Figure 12.1

## Succession Planning Tips

Planning for a successor is full of pitfalls, many of which come from being too close to your own business to see what outsiders see about effecting as smooth a transition as possible. Some thoughts:

1. If you founded your company and run it as an entrepreneur but not as a manager, there's a strong possibility that a manager would make the best replacement. As an entrepreneur, you create value and start new projects, products and services. A manager maximizes the value of those efforts by paying close attention to costs, carefully monitoring time and asset use, and managing the business. Entrepreneurs tend to be poor managers—which is why they start businesses rather than run someone else's.

2. Ask your advisors to help you select a successor. Your banker, accountant, and (if you have one) Board of Directors are obvious sources. Don't ask your employees for suggestions.

3. If your chosen successor isn't ready for the job yet (too young or inexperienced) consider a "caretaker". Some banks provide this  service. If they know your business, then—if worst comes to worst—they can step right in and maintain the value you've spent years creating. A business is never more vulnerable than during periods of transition—when the founder dies or is disabled or retires.

4. A strong management team makes your business more valuable. If you have built a team that can run your business, they may want to buy you out. Terrific—these are people you know and trust, and your investment in them (the paper you will take back)  is more secure than if you or your beneficiaries sell to someone who doesn't know the business.

5. If an outsider wants to buy your business, the same considerations pertain: Now your successor is someone you don't know. If he or she has a trained and experienced team who knows how to keep the business going, not only will you get a better price, but your paper will be more secure.

6. Once you make the decision to leave, set a date and stick to it. You might return once—but after that your credibility is gone. (There's one exception: if the buyer can't follow through and service the debt.) You may be asked to stick around on a part-time or consulting basis. Fine; stick to the terms. Let someone else run the business while you enjoy your retirement.

7. If you have become used to letting employees make decisions (a powerful way to help them grow), letting go is easier. Lead up to it gently if you can—while you still can make the choice.

8. Tapering off beats quitting cold. Maybe your successor would value your help one or two days a week, on a project or consulting basis. Or allow you to use office facilities for personal projects for a while.  If you can put your experience to work easing the transition to new ownership, everyone benefits.

# Appendices One, Two, Three

# Appendix One
# Extra Forms and Checklists

Appendix One contains all the worksheets from the *Personnel Planning Guide*'s text. Please feel free to photocopy these forms for your personal business use. But please respect our copyrights if you wish to reproduce them for republication: Write to Editor, Upstart Publishing Company, Inc., P.O. Box 323, Portsmouth, NH 03801, for permission.

Extra sets may be ordered from Upstart Publishing Company, Inc. Call us toll-free at 800-235-8866 (or 749-5071 in New Hampshire) for current price and delivery information.

# Table of Contents

Figure 2.2

# Task Listing

| Task: | Frequency: | | | |
|---|---|---|---|---|
| | Daily | Weekly | Monthly | Other (specify) |
| 1. | | | | |
| 2. | | | | |
| 3. | | | | |
| 4. | | | | |
| 5. | | | | |
| 6. | | | | |
| 7. | | | | |
| 8. | | | | |
| 9. | | | | |
| 10. | | | | |
| 11. | | | | |
| 12. | | | | |
| 13. | | | | |
| 14. | | | | |
| 15. | | | | |
| 16. | | | | |
| 17. | | | | |
| 18. | | | | |
| 19. | | | | |
| 20. | | | | |

Figure 2.3
# Large Tasks

Name of Task:

People Needed:

What They Do:

When They Do It:     ☐ Daily     ☐ Weekly     ☐ Monthly

                       ☐ Other (Specify) _____

How Many Hours
Does It Take:

Total Time (by Individual
or by Task):

Comments:

Figure 2.4

# Employee Time Use Form

Name of employee:_____

|  | Mon | Tues | Wed | Thurs | Fri | Sat/Sun |
|---|---|---|---|---|---|---|
| 8:00 |  |  |  |  |  |  |
| 8:30 |  |  |  |  |  |  |
| 9:00 |  |  |  |  |  |  |
| 9:30 |  |  |  |  |  |  |
| 10:00 |  |  |  |  |  |  |
| 10:30 |  |  |  |  |  |  |
| 11:00 |  |  |  |  |  |  |
| 11:30 |  |  |  |  |  |  |
| 12:00 |  |  |  |  |  |  |
| 12:30 |  |  |  |  |  |  |
| 1:00 |  |  |  |  |  |  |
| 1:30 |  |  |  |  |  |  |
| 2:00 |  |  |  |  |  |  |
| 2:30 |  |  |  |  |  |  |
| 3:00 |  |  |  |  |  |  |
| 3:30 |  |  |  |  |  |  |
| 4:00 |  |  |  |  |  |  |
| 4:30 |  |  |  |  |  |  |
| 5:00 |  |  |  |  |  |  |
| 5:30 |  |  |  |  |  |  |

Figure 3.1
## Managerial Worksheet

| | Person Responsible | Hours/Week | | Hours/Month | |
|---|---|---|---|---|---|
| | | Actual | Proposed | Actual | Proposed |
| Planning: | | | | | |
| Organizing: | | | | | |
| Staffing: | | | | | |
| Supervising: | | | | | |
| Directing: | | | | | |
| Controlling: | | | | | |
| Coordinating: | | | | | |
| Innovating: | | | | | |

Figure 3.4

# Daily Management Tasks

| Day/ Time | Seek Opportunities | Plan | Organize | Measure | Improve |
|---|---|---|---|---|---|
| Mon. | | | | | |
| Tues. | | | | | |
| Wed. | | | | | |
| Thurs. | | | | | |
| Fri. | | | | | |
| Sat. & Sun. | | | | | |

Figure 3.5
# Task Analysis

| Task | Time Spent Now | Suggested Revisions | Estimated Revised Time |
|------|----------------|---------------------|------------------------|
| 1. | | | |
| 2. | | | |
| 3. | | | |
| 4. | | | |
| 5. | | | |
| 6. | | | |
| 7. | | | |
| 8. | | | |
| 9. | | | |
| 10. | | | |

Figure 3.6
# Time Planning Schedule

| Name _____ Week Ending _____ | |
|---|---|
| Problems/Objectives | Schedule |
| | Monday _____ |
| | _____ |
| | Tuesday _____ |
| | _____ |
| | Wednesday _____ |
| | _____ |
| | Thursday _____ |
| | _____ |
| | Friday _____ |
| | _____ |
| | Saturday _____ |

Figure 4.1

# Employee Planning Form

Position or Name:_____     Date:_____

| Task/Function | Estimated Time | Comments |
|---|---|---|
| 1. | | |
| 2. | | |
| 3. | | |
| 4. | | |
| 5. | | |
| 6. | | |
| 7. | | |
| 8. | | |
| 9. | | |
| 10. | | |
| 11. | | |
| 12. | | |
| 13. | | |
| 14. | | |
| 15. | | |
| 16. | | |
| 17. | | |
| 18. | | |
| 19. | | |
| 20. | | |
| Total Time: | | |

Figure 4.2

# Job Description

Position: _____

Date Prepared: _____

By: _____

| Task/Function | Estimated Hours Per Week |
|---|---|
| 1. | |
| 2. | |
| 3. | |
| 4. | |
| 5. | |
| 6. | |
| 7. | |
| 8. | |
| 9. | |
| 10. | |
| Total Hours: | |

**Job Description:**

**Job Specificatons:**

Comments:

Figure 5.2

## Employee Application Form (Please Print)

Name _____ Social Security No. _____

Street address _____ Apt. no. _____

City _____ State _____ Zip _____

Telephone number _____ Date of birth ___ /___ /___

How did you hear of job? _____

### School Most Recently Attended:

Name _____ Location _____ Phone _____

Graduated? Yes_____ No _____ Now enrolled? Yes _____ No _____ Last grade completed _____

Major _____

### Three Most Recent Jobs:

Company _____ Location _____ Phone _____

Job _____ Supervisor _____ Dates worked: from _____ to _____

Salary _____ Reason for leaving _____

_____

_____

Company _____ Location _____ Phone _____

Job _____ Supervisor _____ Dates worked: from _____ to _____

Salary _____ Reason for leaving _____

_____

_____

Company _____ Location _____ Phone _____

Job _____ Supervisor _____ Dates worked: from _____ to _____

Salary _____ Reason for leaving _____

_____

_____

### U.S. Military

Branch of service _____ Date entered_____ Highest rank held _____

Do you have service-related skills and experience applicable to civilian employment? _____

If yes, describe in full _____

_____

_____

*(continued on next page)*

*(continued from previous page)*

## Physical

Any health problems or physical defects which could affect your employment? Yes_____ No _____

If any such health problems or physical defects exist, please explain _____

_____

During the past 10 years have you ever been convicted of a crime, excluding misdemeanors and traffic violations? Yes _____ No _____ If yes, describe in full _____

_____

_____

## Personal References

(other than family)

Name _____ Telephone number _____

Name _____ Telephone number _____

Name _____ Telephone number _____

Interviewer or reference comments _____

_____

_____

_____

## This Section to Be Filled out by Employer Only After Hire:

Job title _____ Hourly rate _____ Start date____ /___ /_____

Tax status _____ No. of exemptions _____

Person to contact in case of emergency _____

Phone _____

1.  I certify that the information contained in this application is correct to the best of my knowledge and understand that deliberate falsification of this information is grounds for dismissal.

2.  I authorize the references listed above to give you any and all information concerning my previous employment and pertinent information they may have, personal or otherwise, and release all parties from all liability for any damage that may result from furnishing same to you.

3.  I acknowledge that if I become employed, I will be free to resign at any time for any reason, and that management similarly retains the right to terminate my employment at will.

Date _____ Signature _____

Figure 5.3
# Interviewer's Guidelines

**I. Define the interview's purpose beforehand:**
- ☐ Determine ability to do the job.

- ☐ Determine willingness to do the job.

**II. Procedure:**
- ☐ Review application, check references before the interview.

- ☐ Relax applicant.

- ☐ Describe the job as thoroughly as possible.

- ☐ Give applicant a copy of the job description.

- ☐ Ask questions about prior employment: dates, duties, locations.

- ☐ Then ask: likes, dislikes, why he or she left the jobs, what kinds of supervision and working conditions are preferred.

- ☐ Then ask about the applicant's expectations for the job. Look for fits and mismatches with the realities of the job (money, hours, opportunities for growth and advancement, job security and so on).

- ☐ *After eliciting the applicant's expectations:* give information about policies, working conditions, advantages of working for your company, your own expectations for the prospective employee. If you were to present this information sooner, you'd get back an echo: what the applicant thinks you want to hear.

- ☐ Give the applicant your time frame for making the hiring decision.

- ☐ *Do not hire on the spot.* Check references further; get results of physical and skill tests if indicated.

**III. Follow-up:**
- ☐ After applicant leaves: jot down impressions, questions you wished you had asked, thoughts for following up in a further interview. Use Figure 5.6: Selection Summary Sheet.

- ☐ If you decide not to hire the applicant, then tell him/her, explaining only that the applicant who best matched the requirements of the job was hired. The reason to choose one candidate over another is always that the one hired was better matched to the job requirements, even if part of the reason was an adverse reference.

Figure 5.5
## Screening Practices and the Law

Questions you may wish to ask may put you on questionable legal ground.

| | You May: | You May Not: |
|---|---|---|
| Name | Ask for the name (and maiden name) of an applicant, and if he/she was a former employee under another name. | Inquire into the national or religious origin of the name, or ask if it was changed. |
| Address | Ask for the current address and length of residence. | Ask for a past foreign address. |
| Age, Place of Birth | | Ask the applicant's age or date of birth, or require birth certificate, naturalization, or baptismal papers. |
| Religion | | Question the applicant's religion, religious beliefs, parish, names of clergy, or religious holidays observed. |
| Race or Color | | Ask questions relating directly to race or color. |
| Marital Status | Determine if applicant is married, single, divorced or widowed. | |
| Number and Age of Children | Ask the number of dependents. Ask whether they are in school. | Ask age of children or childcare arrangements. |
| Citizenship | Inquire if applicant is a US citizen. If an alien, you may determine if the applicant has permission to remain in the country and has a work permit. | Inquire whether the applicant's spouse or parents are native born or naturalized, or request dates of naturalization or application papers. |
| Education | Obtain names of schools, level of education and graduation dates. | Establish a non-job related educational requirement, or ask the racial, national, or religious affiliation of schools attended. |

*(continued on next page)*

Figure 5.5
*(continued from previous page)*

|  | **You May:** | **You May Not:** |
|---|---|---|
| **Military Service** | Inquire into the applicant's military background, skills learned, and rank attained. | Determine type of discharge, request discharge papers or inquire into the applicant's foreign military service. |
| **Organizations** | Inquire into organizations of which the applicant is a member, providing the organization does not reveal religion, race, color or national origin of its members. You may ask what offices the applicant held. | Request the names of the organizations. |
| **Health-Related** | Determine height, weight, and handicap data. | Set minimum or maximum height, weight, or other physical requirements for the job. |

Figure 5.6
**Selection Summary Sheet**


Date: _____

Interviewer: _____

Position: _____

Candidate's Name: _____

**Comments:**

**"Can Do" Factors:**



**"Will Do" Factors:**



1. Stability:
2. Need for job:
3. Attitude towards supervision:
4. Ability to work with others:
5. Skills and experience:
6. Attitude towards training:
7. Expectations about job:
8. Other factors (specify): _____

_____

_____

Figure 6.1
**Suggestion Form**

Instructions: Write your suggestions clearly, indicating what should be done, why, and how you think it will help the business. If you need more space, or if you need a sketch to make your idea clear, attach extra sheets of paper. All suggestions submitted will be reviewed, and we will keep you informed of the progress of your idea. Thanks.

From: _____ Date:_____

My suggestion is:

It should accomplish:

It will take the following (people, equipment, time, money):

_____

Action Taken:

Discussed with Employee(s) by:_____ Date:_____

Figure 6.3
**Total Compensation**


**Name of Employee**                                                        **Date:**

**During the past quarter, your total compensation included:**

Salary/Wages for quarter:                    $

Social Security paid by company:             $

Workers Compensation premium:                $

Unemployment tax paid:                       $

Other federal, state, local premiums:        $

Health, Accident and Life Insurance:         $

Educational benefits:                        $_____

   **Total**:                                 $

**Other benefits:**
Number of paid vacation days:


Number of paid holidays:


Number of paid sick days:


Number of paid personal days:


Other benefits (specify):

Figure 7.1

**First Day Orientation Form**

Employee name: _____

Position: _____

Date hired: _____ Date started: _____

Person responsible for orientation: _____

Date for review: _____

Employee file opened by: _____ Date: _____

Check box for each item completed.
- ☐ Application received and filed?
- ☐ References checked?
- ☐ Performance test results evaluated and filed?
- ☐ Dates set for evaluation reports:_____ By: _____
- ☐ W4 and Insurance forms given to employee?

**Orientation**
First Day:
- ☐ Welcome
- ☐ Show coatroom, coffee machine, bathroom, other amenities
- ☐ Explain safety regulations
- ☐ Review: working hours, lunch hours, coffee breaks, parking
- ☐ Review job description
- ☐ Describe work
- ☐ Introduce to coworkers
- ☐ Introduce to supervisor
- ☐ Show operation
- ☐ Observe employee perform
- ☐ Review safety rules with employee
- ☐ Let employee know when you are available
- ☐ Check progress at end of first day; ask questions

Figure 7.2
# First Week Orientation Form

Employee name: _____

Position: _____

Reviewed by: _____

Date: _____

Date for next review: _____

At the end of the employee's first week, a brief interview to clarify rules and answer questions about the business is important. Try to get the employee to talk as much as possible—the first week establishes lasting impressions for both of you.

Check off each item after it is discussed.

- ☐ Review job description with employee

- ☐ Review progress

- ☐ Discuss training needs

- ☐ Set performance goals with employee

- ☐ Write down performance goals; give copy to employee

- ☐ Review pay procedures

- ☐ Review benefits (see Figure 6.3)

- ☐ Set date for next review

**Training Needs**

**Comments:** _____

_____

_____

_____

Prepared by: _____

Figure 7.4
**Employee Training Needs**

Name of employee: _____ Date: _____
Reviewed with employee:  ☐ Yes  ☐ No  By: _____

Improvements suggested in these areas:
1.

2.

3.

4.

5.

Suggested solutions:
1.

2.

3.

4.

5.

Training scheduled to start:
1.

2.

3.

4.

5.

Copy to employee. Original to file.

Figure 8.1
# GRAPE Checklist

Bill Scott provides this list of questions to help small business owners understand the elements of his GRAPE theory of management.

1. **Growth**
   - ☐ Do you promote from within whenever possible?
   - ☐ Do you give good recommendations and help employees who leave for better jobs?
   - ☐ Do you train and encourage employees to learn about everything they can?
   - ☐ Do you institute and encourage workshops?
   - ☐ Do you pay partial tuition for schooling related to your company?
   - ☐ Do you counsel and initiate conversations to show employees how to improve or grow or develop a career?
   - ☐ Do you encourage membership in professional clubs or organizations?
   - ☐ Do you publicize promotions?
   - ☐ Do you explain to employees why someone has been brought in from outside? Show them how they can become as well qualified?
   - ☐ Do you rotate jobs among employees?
   - ☐ Do you use flexible work hours?
   - ☐ Do you have a suggestion program?
   - ☐ Do you use meaningful performace evaluations? See Chapter Nine.

2. **Recognition**
   - ☐ Do you know when an employee does an exceptionally good job—and let him or her know you know?
   - ☐ Do you know your employees' hobbies, interests, needs, and goals?
   - ☐ Do you provide time to listen to individual employees?
   - ☐ Do you meet with each employee for performance evaluations?
   - ☐ Do you ask employees to help improve business operations?
   - ☐ Do you help employees improve their skills?

3. **Achievement**
   - ☐ Do you allow your employees chances to excel? To do the job their way?
   - ☐ Do you explain what you want accomplished and allow your employees to figure out how to achieve those goals?
   - ☐ Do you set assignments that stretch employees' abilities?
   - ☐ Do you think your employees are capable of doing more or better work?
   - ☐ Do you provide the tools, time, and other resources to improve their performance?
   - ☐ Do you applaud their off-work achievements?
   - ☐ Do you allow employees to use their heads in achieving your goals?

4. **Participation**
   - ☐ Do you ask your employees' advice? Solicit their opinions?
   - ☐ Do you implement their suggestions?
   - ☐ Do you encourage employees to speak up?
   - ☐ Do you practice listening?
   - ☐ Can employees shape their work environment to some degree: hours, work groups, plants or pictures and so on?
   - ☐ Do you use Management by Objectives? (MBO: See Chapter Nine.)

## Figure 9.1
## **Employee Performance Evaluation**

Review period    From: _____ To: _____

Employee's name: _____

Position: _____

Review prepared by: _____ Date of review: _____

---

**Quality of Work:** Consider the degree to which the employee produces accurate, neat, and thorough work:

| ☐ | ☐ | ☐ | ☐ | ☐ |
|---|---|---|---|---|
| Consistently produces work of highest quality. | Frequently produces high quality work; makes few errors. | Produces acceptable work. | Produces marginally acceptable work; makes more than an average number of errors. | Produces unacceptable work; makes excessive errors. |

Comments: _____

_____

---

**Quantity of Work:** Consider the employee's level of productivity/output and timeliness of work:

| ☐ | ☐ | ☐ | ☐ | ☐ |
|---|---|---|---|---|
| Consistently exceeds productivity requirements; consistently completes work ahead of schedule; highest level of output. | Frequently exceeds basic productivity requirements; frequently completes work ahead of schedule; above average level of output. | Meets basic productivity requirements; meets deadlines; acceptable level of output. | Below basic productivity requirements; slow worker, often misses deadlines; marginal level of output. | Fails to meet basic productivity requirements; misses deadlines; unsatisfactory level of output. |

Comments: _____

_____

---

**Working Relationships:** Consider the employee's ability to work with others:

| ☐ | ☐ | ☐ | ☐ | ☐ |
|---|---|---|---|---|
| Consistently achieves outstanding working relationships. | Helps to create a cooperative work environment; good team worker. | Cooperative; usually works well with others. | Sometimes cooperative; occasionally experiences difficulty relating to others. | Uncooperative; cannot work with others. |

Comments: _____

_____

## Supervision Required: Consider the amount of direction and supervision the employee requires:

| ☐ | ☐ | ☐ | ☐ | ☐ |
|---|---|---|---|---|
| Requires little or no direction or supervision, even on non-routine assignments. | Requires less than normal direction or supervision, even on non-routine assignments. | Requires normal direction and supervision on routine assignments. Requires assistance on non-routine assignments. | Requires more than normal direction and supervision to complete assignments. | Requires constant direction and supervision to complete assignments. |

Comments: _____

_____

_____

## Objective Achievement: Consider the employee's ability to achieve objectives and adjust to changing circumstances on time:

| ☐ | ☐ | ☐ | ☐ |
|---|---|---|---|
| Consistently outstanding in achieving objectives ahead of schedule; performance is of the highest caliber. | Frequently achieves objectives ahead of schedule; performance is well above job standard. | Achieves objectives satisfactorily and on schedule. | Sometimes unable to achieve objectives and/or meet deadlines due to poor judgment or lack of foresight. |

Comments: _____

_____

_____

## Problem-Solving Skills: Consider the employee's ability to recognize and analyze problems and then to evaluate solutions and make recommendations:

| ☐ | ☐ | ☐ | ☐ |
|---|---|---|---|
| Consistently demonstrates outstanding problem solving skills; handles complex problems thoroughly. | Frequently demonstrates average problem solving skills; occasionally able to handle complex problems. | Solves routine problems satisfactorily; requires assistance on complex problems. | Sometimes has difficulty in recognizing and solving routine problems; analytical skills need improvement. |

Comments: _____

_____

_____

**Initiative:** Consider the degree to which the employee demonstrates independent action and resourcefulness on the job by developing new methods, offering constructive suggestions, and/or seeking additional work:

| ☐ | ☐ | ☐ | ☐ |
|---|---|---|---|
| Consistently exceeds basic requirements for independent action and resourcefulness; highly motivated. | Frequently exceeds basic requirements for independent action and resourcefulness; diligent worker. | Meets basic job requirements for independent action and resourcefulness; acceptable worker. | Sometimes lacks independent action and resourcefulness required by job; marginal worker. |

Comments: _____

_____

_____

**Verbal Communications Skills:** Consider the employee's ability to verbally express ideas clearly and convincingly:

| ☐ | ☐ | ☐ | ☐ |
|---|---|---|---|
| Consistently demonstrates excellent communications skills. | Frequently demonstrates above average communications skills. | Demonstrates acceptable communications skills. | Communications skills need improvement. |

Comments: _____

_____

_____

**Written Communication Skills:** Consider the employee's ability to express ideas in writing clearly and convincingly:

| ☐ | ☐ | ☐ | ☐ |
|---|---|---|---|
| Consistently demonstrates excellent communications skills. | Frequently demonstrates above average communications skills. | Demonstrates acceptable communications skills. | Communications skills need improvement. |

Comments: _____

_____

_____

## Overall Performance Rating

| Superior | Above Average | Satisfactory | Marginal/ Needs Improvement | Unsatisfactory |
|:---:|:---:|:---:|:---:|:---:|
| ☐ | ☐ | ☐ | ☐ | ☐ |

What are the employee's main strengths?

In what areas does the employee need improvement?

## Potential

I understand that my signature below indicates only that I have read and discussed this performance evaluation with my supervisor/evaluator; this does not necessarily constitute my agreement with this evaluation's contents.

Employee's signature: _____ Date: _____

Supervisor/
evaluator's signature: _____ Date: _____

After completing the form, conduct a formal performance review session with the employee. Communicate standards for quality and quantity of work so the employee can understand the measurement criteria used in the evaluation. Both you and the employee should sign the form. The employee's signature does not necessarily indicate agreement with the evaluation. It merely indicates that the performance appraisal has been seen and discussed with the employee.

The form becomes part of the employee's file.

Figure 9.2
# Preliminary Goal Setting

**I.  Performance Objectives: Employee Preliminary Goals**
Employee: _____ Date proposed: _____

For period: _____ to _____ To be reviewed: _____

Basic job description (Attach copy if available):

_____

_____

_____

_____

_____

_____

**II.  Objectives I Can Realistically Accomplish**
(Example:100% accuracy is not realistic; improvement from 90% accuracy to 95% may be.)

1. _____
2. _____
3. _____
4. _____
5. _____
6. _____
7. _____
8. _____

**III. Measurement of Success**
(Example: Dollar amount, hours, percentages of measurable quantities, averages.)

1. _____
2. _____
3. _____
4. _____
5. _____
6. _____
7. _____
8. _____

**IV. In Order to Accomplish These Objectives I Need the Following:**
(Examples: additional tools, time, money, training, personnel and so forth.)

1. _____
2. _____
3. _____
4. _____
5. _____
6. _____
7. _____
8. _____

Figure 9.3
**Performance Appraisal**

Employee name: _____ Date: _____

**Objective:**                           **Results:**                     **Comments:**

## Figure 10.1
## Disciplinary Guidelines

| Incident | Offense | | | |
|---|---|---|---|---|
| | **First** | **Second** | **Third** | **Fourth** |
| 1. Absent, no call | | | | |
| 2. Walking off job, no reason or notice given | | | | |
| 3. Arguing with employee(s) | | | | |
| 4. Arguing with customer | | | | |
| 5. Fighting with employee or fighting with customer | | | | |
| 6. Intimidation, harassment (sexual or other) of employee | | | | |
| 7. Insubordination | | | | |
| 8. Purposeful destruction of company property | | | | |
| 9. Theft | | | | |
| 10. Possession or sale of illegal drugs or alcohol on company property | | | | |
| 11. Intoxication or being under the influence of illegal drugs on company property | | | | |
| 12. Ignoring safety rules | | | | |

**Key:**  O = oral reminder     W = written reminder         SP = suspend with pay
SW = suspend without pay    F = fire

Fill in the appropriate blanks for your business.

Figure 10.2

# Handling a Problem Employee

Follow this checklist when a problem arises that you think will lead to progressively more serious disciplinary actions. Keep notes—with dates— to substantiate the content of discussions and counseling efforts.
**Name of employee:**

**Describe behavior(s):**

**Date, Initials**

☐ Employee notified of performance and behavior standards _____

☐ Oral reminders _____

For minor incidents, use oral reminders immediately. Don't store grievances. Solve the problem instead. Collect and evaluate facts—not feelings or assumptions—and make notes covering dates and results.

If the problem persists for a single moderate incident or if the employee fails to respond to several oral reminders:

☐ State the violation clearly, in writing, with dates, names, facts (no hearsay, anger, or phrases which could be interpreted as insults). Review with the offending employee, get his/her signature, give him/her a copy, and keep the original for your files.

The next step is either a suspension or a final written notice. Reserve this for either a single incident of severe misconduct or for a final warning to improve.

☐ Advise the person that his or her job and income are in immediate danger.
☐ Suspend with pay if the facts are in doubt; investigate thoroughly.
☐ Give the employee a copy of the final written notice. Keep the original for your files.

If it is necessary to fire the employee:

☐ Make sure to have a valid business reason, based on facts and documented to make sure the procedure has been fair.
☐ If there is any doubt, ask your lawyer's advice.
☐ Prepare the paperwork: last paycheck, other personnel documents (such as insurance notification). Be sure your records illustrate the steps taken as outlined above.
☐ Prepare for the exit interview. See Figure 10.3. It is often advisable to have another person present. Select the time and place for privacy.
☐ Notify the employee. Ordinarily he or she is expecting to be fired, but be prepared for either anger or tears. Keep it businesslike, make it final, and notify them of any appeal procedure they might follow. In a small business where you are the appeal procedure, this is still important. Let the employee respond.
☐ Finish off all loose ends: Arrange return of company keys, and other property; explain severance pay and insurance procedures.

Your objective remains the same: to treat this employee fairly and to show that you made every reasonable effort to remedy the problem. Do this, and you're probably legally covered. ("Probably" is underlined as a warning: As mentioned earlier, courts take somewhat erratic views. When in any doubt at all, check with your lawyer.)

Figure 10.3
## Exit Interview

Employee _____  Title _____
Last day worked _____
Please check the following appropriately:

| | Excellent | Good | Fair | Poor | Comments |
|---|---|---|---|---|---|
| 1. How were our working conditions? | ☐ | ☐ | ☐ | ☐ | |
| 2. How was your compensation? | ☐ | ☐ | ☐ | ☐ | |
| 3. How well are tasks and employees matched? | ☐ | ☐ | ☐ | ☐ | |
| 4. How well was work organized? | ☐ | ☐ | ☐ | ☐ | |
| 5. What did you feel your growth potential was? | ☐ | ☐ | ☐ | ☐ | |
| 6. What did you feel your opportunity was to participate, make suggestions, be involved in your work? | ☐ | ☐ | ☐ | ☐ | |
| 7. How well did you receive recognition or credit for your contributions? | ☐ | ☐ | ☐ | ☐ | |
| 8. How did management treat you? | ☐ | ☐ | ☐ | ☐ | |

9. My major reason for leaving is:_____
_____
_____
_____

10. Can you make any suggestions as to how the company could be a better place in which to work?
_____
_____
_____
_____

11. Remarks: _____
_____
_____
_____

Forwarding Address: _____
_____
_____

Date _____  Company representative interviewing employee _____

# Appendix Two

# Bibliography and Resources

# Bibliography

There are many excellent texts available on small-business management, but most are more appropriate for businesses with more than 100 employees. Check out your local library, college bookstores, and these sources of small-business management information:

1. **Upstart Publishing Company, Inc.:** *Profit Improvement Guides.* This series of handbooks on proven management techniques for small businesses is available from Upstart Publishing Company, Inc., 12 Portland Street, Dover, NH 03820. For a free current catalogue, call 800-235-8866 outside New Hampshire or 749-5071 in state.

   The series consists of the following books:

   *Business Planning Guide*, © 1976, 1985, 1988, David H. Bangs, Jr. and Upstart Publishing Company, Inc. A 160-page manual that helps you write a business plan and financing proposal tailored to your business, your goals, and your resources. Includes worksheets and checklists.

   *Personnel Planning Guide*, © 1988, David H. Bangs, Jr. and Upstart Publishing Company, Inc. A 160-page manual outlining practical and proven personnel management techniques, including hiring, managing, evaluating and compensating personnel. Includes worksheets and checklists.

   *Cash Flow Control Guide*, © 1988, David H. Bangs, Jr. and Upstart Publishing Company, Inc. A 75-page manual to help small-business owners solve their number-one financial problem. Includes worksheets and checklists.

   *Market Planning Guide*, © 1988, David H. Bangs, Jr. and Upstart Publishing Company, Inc. A 240-page manual to help small-business owners put together a goal-oriented, resource-based marketing plan with action steps, benchmarks, and timelines. Includes worksheets and checklists to make implementation and review easier.

   *How to Earn More Profits Through the People Who Work for You*, William H. Scott, © 1982, Prentice-Hall. Currently out of print, but available from Bill Scott, c/o Upstart Publishing Co., Inc., 12 Portland Street, Dover, NH 03820. $7.95/copy, shipping & handling included.

   *Common Sense Management Techniques.* These six-page, in-depth reports focus on various aspects of running a small business, and are published by Upstart Publishing Co., Inc., 12 Portland Street, Dover, NH 03820. Topics are updated on a regular basis, and currently over 60 are available. Titles include *Inventory Management, Choosing the Right Computer, Estate Planning and the Closely-Held Business, Developing a Personnel Manual,* and more. Each report costs $4.95. For a list of available and upcoming topics, call 800-235-8866 outside New Hampshire or 749-5071 in state.

2. *Small Business Reporter.* An excellent series of booklets on small-business management published by Bank of America, Department 3120, PO Box 37000, San Francisco, CA 94137. 1-415-622-2491. Individual copies are $5 each. Ask for a list of current titles—they have about 17 available including, *Steps to Starting a Business, Avoiding Management Pitfalls, Business Financing* and *Marketing Small Business.*

3. *In Business.* A bimonthly magazine for small businesses, especially those with less than 10 employees. The publisher is J.G. Press, PO Box 323, Emmaus, PA, 18049. Annual subscriptions are $18.

4. ***The Great Brain Robbery***, Ray Considine and Murray Raphel, © 1980, 1981, by The Great Brain Robbery, 1360 East Rubio Street, Altadena, CA 91101. Subtitled "A collection of proven ideas to make you money and change your life!," *The Great Brain Robbery* contains numerous checklists and ideas which are thought-provoking. The chapters entitled "Formula for Success," "Secret Selling Sentences," and "If You Don't Like It Here, Get Out!" are particularly provocative. Raphel and Considine are marketing and promotional experts—which is apparent throughout this book.

5. ***Marketing with Facts***, © 1986, published by Price Waterhouse, 1251 Avenue of the Americas, New York, NY 10020. This book, part of a series aimed at small-business owners and entrepreneurs, focuses on how marketing information can be used to enhance opportunities for profit. The book's lists of questions and lexicon of marketing terminology are particularly helpful. Copies of this book cost $5.00 and are available at any Price Waterhouse office.

# Resources

1. **Small Business Development Centers** (SBDCs). Call your state university or the Small Business Administration (SBA) to find the SBDC nearest to you. One of the best free management program available, SBDCs provide expert assistance and training in every aspect of business management. Don't ignore this resource.

2. **SCORE,** or Service Corps of Retired Executives, sponsored by the U.S. Small Business Administration, provides free counseling and also a series of workshops and seminars for small businesses. There are over 500 chapters nationwide. For more information contact the SBA office nearest you and ask for SCORE.

3. **Small Business Administration** (SBA). Besides the numerous lending programs, the SBA has a number of management assistance programs. These programs are subject to frequent change due to Congressional mandates and budgetary requirements. The SBA also co-sponsors many workshops and seminars and has an extensive library of small business literature. The SBA is listed in the white pages of your phone book under "U.S. Government."

4. **Colleges and universities.** Most have business courses. Some have SBDCs, others have more specialized programs. Some have small-business expertise—the University of New Hampshire, for example, has two schools which provide direct small-business management assistance.

5. **Keye Productivity Center,** P.O. Box 23192, Kansas City, MO 64141. Keye Productivity offers business seminars on specific personnel topics for a reasonable fee. Call them at 800-821-3919 for topics and prices. Their seminar entitled *Hiring and Firing* is excellent, well-documented, and useful. Good handout materials are included.

6. **Comprehensive Accounting Corporation,** 2111 Comprehensive Drive, Aurora, IL 60507. CAC has over 425 franchised offices providing accounting, bookkeeping and management consulting services to small businesses. For information, call 800-323-9009.

7. **General Business Services,** 20271 Goldenrod Lane, Germantown, MD 20874-4090. GBS has nearly 1,000 franchised offices providing accounting, bookkeeping and management consulting services to small businesses. For information, call 301-428-1040.

8. **Center for Entrepreneurial Management,** 180 Varick Street, New York, NY 10014. The oldest and largest nonprofit membership association for small-business owners in the world. They maintain an extensive list of books, videotapes, cassettes and other small-business management aids. Call 212-633-0060 for information.

9. **Libraries.** Do not forget to take advantage of the information that is readily available at your library.

# Appendix Three

# Why Your Company Needs a Personnel Manual

# Why Your Company Needs a Personnel Manual

*"I was recently in a seminar in which the instructor asked, 'How many of you can conceive of going to court against an employee?' (About 90% raised their hands.) 'How many of you have a current, written, personnel manual?' (About 5% raised their hands.) 'This,' he said, patting a copy of his company's manual, 'is what lawyers call evidence.'"*

> —Jean Kerr, Vice President, Upstart Publishing Company, Inc.

Personnel manuals set down company policies, clarify the respective roles of employer and employee, and help you avoid a lot of personnel problems.

If you don't have a personnel manual, make sure to involve your employees when you write one—the unwritten rules and practices of a business cannot be changed by fiat, but if your employees help define the written rules and practices, significant changes can be effected. For instance, if you have been lax about working hours, with some employees coming in at 7, and some at 9:30, you can't suddenly say "We have work hours of 9 to 4:30," and expect your employees to cooperate.

What should an employee manual contain? The following is a checklist of the most common subjects covered in a personnel manual. They aren't listed in any special order, nor does each item apply to every business. Use them as guidelines for the typical matters to consider when setting up a personnel manual.

Have your lawyer check the suggested phrases used as examples in the checklist.

**Welcome:** A short statement of company values and philosophy.

**Introduction/history of company:** Brag about your business, instill a sense of pride and participation. What's special or unique about your business? Products? People? Service? Quality? Customers?

**Equal Opportunity Statement:** "We are an equal opportunity employer. Qualifications for employment and promotion are based solely upon your ability to do the job, and also upon your dependability and reliability once hired. Race, color, religion, sex, national origin and age are not considered in hiring, employment, benefits, or advancement opportunities. The only factors that will affect the hiring decisions are bona fide occupational qualifications."

**Sexual harassment policy:** "All employees have the right to a work environment free from intimidation and harassment. This company prohibits any act, physical, verbal, or visual, that has the effect of unreasonably interfering with the employee's work performance, or creates an intimidating, hostile, or offensive work atmosphere. An employee should immediately report any complaints to the owner."

**Job application form.**

**Operating procedures:**
- ☐ Employee classifications (define full-time, part-time)
- ☐ Payroll
- ☐ Working hours
- ☐ Probationary period
- ☐ Performance reviews
- ☐ Salary reviews
- ☐ Use of company property and equipment

**Management rights:** "The company retains the exclusive right to hire, direct and schedule the working force; to plan, direct, and control operations; to discontinue, reorganize, or combine any department or branch of operations; to hire, terminate, and lay off employees; to announce rules and regulations; and in all respects carry out the ordinary and customary functions of management.

"It is the company's intent to grow and prosper, but it is recognized that all policies, benefits, procedures, and/or operating methods are subject to change or discontinuation at the option of management.

"None of these rights will be exercised in an unreasonable manner."

**Employee benefits:**
- ☐ Insurance
- ☐ Vacations/holidays/sick leave
- ☐ Personal days ("mental health days")
- ☐ Pension plan
- ☐ Education allowance
- ☐ Leave of absence
- ☐ Military leave
- ☐ Jury duty
- ☐ Workers compensation

**Employee obligations:**
- ☐ Relationship to management
- ☐ Performance
- ☐ Attendance
- ☐ Discussion of company affairs or secrets
- ☐ Dress code
- ☐ Disciplinary and grievance procedures
- ☐ Resignations

**Other information:**
- ☐ Safety rules and regulations
- ☐ Location of fire extinguishers, first aid box, etc.
- ☐ List of emergency phone numbers
- ☐ Names of employees trained in CPR or First Aid.

Modify this to suit your business needs. You may want employees to sign a release indicating that they have read and understand the manual—but make sure that is legal in your state.

# Notes